# 100 Chocolate Recipes for Home

By: Kelly Johnson

**Table of Contents**

Recipes
- Classic Chocolate Chip Cookies
- Dark Chocolate Truffles
- Chocolate Lava Cake
- White Chocolate Raspberry Cheesecake
- Chocolate Covered Strawberries
- Chocolate Mousse
- Triple Chocolate Brownies
- Chocolate Banana Bread
- Chocolate Dipped Pretzels
- Nutella Chocolate Milkshake
- Mint Chocolate Chip Ice Cream
- Chocolate Pots de Creme
- Chocolate Covered Nuts
- Chocolate Tiramisu
- Chocolate Zucchini Bread
- Mexican Hot Chocolate
- Chocolate Covered Oreos
- Chocolate Soufflé
- Chocolate Coconut Macaroons
- Chocolate Espresso Martini
- Chocolate Covered Caramel Apples
- Chocolate Fondue
- Chocolate Pecan Pie

- Chocolate Hazelnut Biscotti
- Chocolate Avocado Mousse
- Chocolate Raspberry Tart
- White Chocolate Macadamia Nut Cookies
- Chocolate Peanut Butter Cups
- Dark Chocolate Almond Bark
- Chocolate Pudding
- Chocolate Orange Trifle
- Chocolate Cherry Smoothie
- Chocolate Pretzel Bark
- Chocolate Mint Brownies
- Chocolate Caramel Popcorn
- Chocolate Pistachio Torte
- Chocolate Hazelnut Spread
- Chocolate Raspberry Cupcakes
- Rocky Road Chocolate Bars
- Chocolate Almond Jooy Bites
- Chocolate Cinnamon Rolls
- Chocolate Covered Cherry Cheesecake
- Chocolate Strawberry Shortcake
- Chocolate Bread Pudding
- Chocolate Peppermint Bark
- Chocolate Toffee Crunch Cookies
- Chocolate Pumpkin Pie
- Chocolate Marshmallow Fudge
- Chocolate Raspberry Scones
- Chocolate Pecan Pie Bars

- Chocolate Espresso Brownies
- Chocolate Caramel Brownie Trifle
- Chocolate Pistachio Ice Cream
- Chocolate Hazelnut Cookies
- Chocolate Raspberry Pancakes
- Chocolate Coconut Truffles
- Chocolate Covered Banana Bites
- Chocolate Mint Ice Cream Sandwiches
- Chocolate Cherry Galette
- Chocolate Orange Biscotti
- Chocolate Strawberry Tartlets
- Chocolate Almond Butter Cups
- Chocolate Coconut Chia Pudding
- Chocolate Walnut Blondies
- Chocolate Raspberry Bread Pudding
- Chocolate Walnut Blondies
- Chocolate Raspberry Bread Pudding
- Chocolate Caramel Pretzel Bars
- Chocolate Peanut Butter Banana Smoothie
- Chocolate Toffee Cheesecake
- Chocolate Hazelnut Croissants
- Chocolate Raspberry Chia Seed Pudding
- Chocolate Mint Cheesecake
- Chocolate Almond Flourless Cake
- Chocolate Cherry Clafoutis
- Chocolate Orange Scones
- Chocolate Raspberry Crepes

- Chocolate Peanut Butter Energy Bites
- Chocolate Covered Blueberries
- Chocolate Pecan Caramel Rolls
- Chocolate Hazelnut Muffins
- Chocolate raspberry Almond Cake
- Chocolate Coconut Ice Cream
- Chocolate Covered Macadamia Nuts
- Chocolate Banana Pancakes
- Chocolate Mint Oreo Truffles
- Chocolate Hazelnut Pancakes
- Chocolate Raspberry Ice Cream
- Chocolate Almond Joy Smoothie
- Chocolate Tiramisu Cupcakes
- Chocolate Coconut Cream Pie
- Chocolate Raspberry Danish
- Chocolate Mint Thumbprint Cookies
- Chocolate Pecan Pie Milkshake
- Chocolate Hazelnut Cheesecake
- Chocolate Cherry Almond Granola
- Chocolate Orange Ricotta Pancakes
- Chocolate Raspberry Popsicles
- Chocolate Banana Split
- Chocolate Mint Panna Cotta
- Chocolate Pecan Pralines
- Chocolate Hazelnut Granola Bars

**Classic Chocolate Chip Cookies**

*Ingredients:*

- 1 cup (2 sticks) unsalted butter, softened
- 3/4 cup granulated sugar
- 3/4 cup packed brown sugar
- 2 large eggs
- 1 teaspoon vanilla extract
- 2 1/4 cups all-purpose flour
- 1 teaspoon baking soda
- 1/2 teaspoon salt
- 2 cups semisweet chocolate chips
- 1 cup chopped nuts (optional)

*Instructions:*

Preheat your oven to 375°F (190°C) and line baking sheets with parchment paper.
In a large mixing bowl, cream together the softened butter, granulated sugar, and brown sugar until smooth and creamy.
Beat in the eggs one at a time, ensuring each is fully incorporated. Stir in the vanilla extract.
In a separate bowl, whisk together the all-purpose flour, baking soda, and salt.
Gradually add the dry ingredients to the wet ingredients, mixing just until combined.
Fold in the chocolate chips and nuts (if using) until evenly distributed in the dough.
Drop rounded tablespoons of dough onto the prepared baking sheets, spacing them about 2 inches apart.
Bake in the preheated oven for 9-11 minutes or until the edges are golden but the centers are still soft.
Allow the cookies to cool on the baking sheets for a few minutes before transferring them to a wire rack to cool completely.
Enjoy your classic chocolate chip cookies with a glass of milk or your favorite beverage!

Feel free to customize this recipe based on your preferences, and don't forget to include any special tips or variations in your cookbook. Happy baking!

**Dark Chocolate Truffles**

*Ingredients:*

- 8 oz (about 1 1/3 cups) dark chocolate, finely chopped
- 1/2 cup heavy cream
- 2 tablespoons unsalted butter, softened
- 1 teaspoon vanilla extract
- Cocoa powder, chopped nuts, or shredded coconut for coating (optional)

*Instructions:*

Place the finely chopped dark chocolate in a heatproof bowl.
In a small saucepan, heat the heavy cream over medium heat until it just begins to simmer. Do not boil.
Pour the hot cream over the chopped chocolate. Let it sit for a minute to melt the chocolate, and then gently stir until smooth and well combined.
Add the softened butter and vanilla extract to the chocolate mixture. Stir until the butter is fully incorporated.
Cover the bowl with plastic wrap and refrigerate the chocolate mixture for at least 2 hours, or until it is firm enough to handle.
Once the chocolate mixture is firm, use a spoon or a melon baller to scoop out small portions and roll them into bite-sized truffle balls.
If desired, roll the truffles in cocoa powder, chopped nuts, or shredded coconut to coat them.
Place the coated truffles on a parchment-lined tray and refrigerate for an additional 30 minutes to set.
Serve the dark chocolate truffles chilled and enjoy the rich, decadent flavor!

These dark chocolate truffles make for a delightful treat and can be a perfect addition to any special occasion or as a homemade gift. Feel free to experiment with different coatings or add a touch of liqueur for flavor variation. Include any tips or suggestions in your cookbook for a personal touch. Enjoy!

**Chocolate Lava Cake**

*Ingredients:*

- 1/2 cup (1 stick) unsalted butter
- 4 oz semi-sweet chocolate, chopped
- 1 cup powdered sugar
- 2 large eggs
- 2 egg yolks
- 1 teaspoon vanilla extract
- 1/4 cup all-purpose flour
- Pinch of salt
- Cocoa powder or powdered sugar for dusting (optional)
- Vanilla ice cream for serving (optional)

*Instructions:*

Preheat your oven to 425°F (220°C). Grease and flour individual ramekins or custard cups.
In a heatproof bowl, melt the butter and chopped chocolate together. You can do this using a double boiler or in short bursts in the microwave. Stir until smooth.
Stir in the powdered sugar until well combined.
Add the eggs and egg yolks one at a time, beating well after each addition.
Stir in the vanilla extract.
Gently fold in the flour and a pinch of salt until just combined. Be careful not to overmix.
Divide the batter evenly among the prepared ramekins.
Place the ramekins on a baking sheet and bake in the preheated oven for 12-14 minutes. The edges should be set, but the center should still be soft.
Remove the lava cakes from the oven and let them cool for a minute. Carefully run a knife around the edges to loosen the cakes.
Invert each lava cake onto a serving plate. Dust with cocoa powder or powdered sugar if desired.
Serve immediately, optionally with a scoop of vanilla ice cream for an extra indulgent treat.

Enjoy the decadent and gooey center of these chocolate lava cakes! Make sure to note in your cookbook the importance of timing for that perfect molten center. It's a delightful dessert for any chocolate lover.

**White Chocolate Raspberry Cheesecake**

*Ingredients:*

For the Crust:

- 1 1/2 cups graham cracker crumbs
- 1/4 cup granulated sugar
- 1/2 cup unsalted butter, melted

For the Cheesecake Filling:

- 24 oz cream cheese, softened
- 1 cup granulated sugar
- 3 large eggs
- 1 teaspoon vanilla extract
- 1 cup white chocolate chips, melted and cooled
- 1/2 cup sour cream
- 1/2 cup raspberry preserves or fresh raspberries

For the Raspberry Sauce:

- 1 cup fresh or frozen raspberries
- 1/4 cup granulated sugar
- 1 tablespoon lemon juice

*Instructions:*

For the Crust:

> Preheat your oven to 325°F (163°C). Grease a 9-inch springform pan.
> In a bowl, combine graham cracker crumbs, sugar, and melted butter. Press the mixture into the bottom of the prepared pan.
> Bake the crust in the preheated oven for 10 minutes. Remove and allow it to cool while preparing the filling.

For the Cheesecake Filling:

> In a large mixing bowl, beat the softened cream cheese until smooth.
> Add sugar and continue to beat until well combined.

Add eggs one at a time, beating well after each addition. Stir in the vanilla extract.
Fold in the melted white chocolate until evenly distributed.
Finally, fold in the sour cream until smooth.
Pour half of the cheesecake batter over the crust.
Spoon dollops of raspberry preserves or fresh raspberries over the batter.
Pour the remaining cheesecake batter over the raspberries, spreading it evenly.
Use a knife to gently swirl the raspberries into the batter for a marbled effect.

For the Raspberry Sauce:

In a small saucepan, combine raspberries, sugar, and lemon juice.
Cook over medium heat until the raspberries break down and the mixture thickens slightly.
Remove from heat and strain the sauce to remove seeds. Allow it to cool.

Assembling and Baking:

Pour the raspberry sauce over the top of the cheesecake batter.
Use a toothpick or skewer to create swirl patterns on the surface.
Bake the cheesecake in the preheated oven for 55-60 minutes or until the center is set.
Allow the cheesecake to cool in the oven with the door ajar for about an hour.
Refrigerate the cheesecake for at least 4 hours or overnight before serving.
Once chilled, remove the cheesecake from the springform pan, slice, and serve.

This White Chocolate Raspberry Cheesecake is a luscious combination of creamy white chocolate and the tartness of raspberries. It's perfect for special occasions or as a delightful dessert. Enjoy!

**Chocolate Covered Strawberries**

*Ingredients:*

- Fresh strawberries, washed and dried
- 8 oz (about 1 1/3 cups) semisweet or dark chocolate, chopped
- White chocolate for drizzling (optional)
- Toppings (optional): chopped nuts, shredded coconut, sprinkles

*Instructions:*

Line a baking sheet with parchment paper.
In a heatproof bowl, melt the semisweet or dark chocolate. You can use a double boiler or microwave in short bursts, stirring frequently until smooth.
Hold each strawberry by the stem and dip it into the melted chocolate, covering it about three-quarters of the way up. Allow excess chocolate to drip back into the bowl.
Place the chocolate-covered strawberry on the prepared baking sheet. Repeat with the remaining strawberries.
If desired, melt white chocolate and drizzle it over the dipped strawberries for a decorative touch.
While the chocolate is still wet, you can sprinkle the strawberries with your choice of toppings such as chopped nuts, shredded coconut, or sprinkles.
Allow the chocolate-covered strawberries to set at room temperature or, for faster setting, place them in the refrigerator for about 30 minutes.
Once the chocolate is fully set, transfer the strawberries to a serving plate.
Serve and enjoy these delightful chocolate-covered strawberries as a sweet treat or as a beautiful dessert for special occasions.

Feel free to get creative with the toppings or even try using different types of chocolate for dipping. Include any tips for achieving the perfect chocolate coating in your cookbook. These chocolate-covered strawberries are a classic and elegant treat that's sure to be a crowd-pleaser!

**Chocolate Mousse**

*Ingredients:*

- 8 oz (about 1 1/3 cups) semisweet chocolate, chopped
- 1/4 cup unsalted butter
- 3 large eggs, separated
- 1/4 cup granulated sugar
- 1 teaspoon vanilla extract
- 1 cup heavy cream
- Whipped cream and chocolate shavings for garnish (optional)

*Instructions:*

In a heatproof bowl, melt the chopped semisweet chocolate and butter together. You can use a double boiler or melt in the microwave in short bursts, stirring frequently until smooth. Allow it to cool slightly.
In a separate bowl, whisk together the egg yolks, sugar, and vanilla extract until well combined.
Gradually whisk the melted chocolate mixture into the egg yolk mixture until smooth.
In a clean, dry bowl, whip the egg whites until stiff peaks form.
Gently fold the whipped egg whites into the chocolate mixture until no white streaks remain.
In another bowl, whip the heavy cream until soft peaks form.
Fold the whipped cream into the chocolate mixture until well combined and smooth.
Divide the chocolate mousse into serving glasses or ramekins.
Refrigerate the mousse for at least 2 hours, or until set.
If desired, garnish with a dollop of whipped cream and chocolate shavings before serving.
Serve and enjoy the creamy and indulgent chocolate mousse!

This chocolate mousse is a classic dessert that's rich, silky, and absolutely delightful. Feel free to experiment with different garnishes or serve it on its own for an elegant treat. Include any helpful tips for achieving the perfect texture in your cookbook. Enjoy!

**Triple Chocolate Brownies**

*Ingredients:*

For the Brownies:

- 1 cup (2 sticks) unsalted butter
- 1 1/2 cups granulated sugar
- 4 large eggs
- 1 teaspoon vanilla extract
- 1 cup all-purpose flour
- 1/2 cup cocoa powder
- 1/4 teaspoon salt
- 1 cup semisweet chocolate chips
- 1 cup white chocolate chips
- 1 cup milk chocolate chips

For the Chocolate Ganache:

- 1/2 cup heavy cream
- 1 cup semisweet chocolate chips

*Instructions:*

For the Brownies:

>Preheat your oven to 350°F (175°C). Grease a 9x13-inch baking pan.
>In a saucepan, melt the butter over low heat. Remove from heat and let it cool slightly.
>In a large mixing bowl, combine the melted butter and sugar. Mix well.
>Add the eggs one at a time, beating well after each addition. Stir in the vanilla extract.
>In a separate bowl, whisk together the flour, cocoa powder, and salt.
>Gradually add the dry ingredients to the wet ingredients, mixing until just combined.
>Fold in the semisweet chocolate chips, white chocolate chips, and milk chocolate chips.
>Spread the batter evenly into the prepared baking pan.
>Bake in the preheated oven for 25-30 minutes or until a toothpick inserted into the center comes out with a few moist crumbs.

Allow the brownies to cool completely in the pan on a wire rack.

For the Chocolate Ganache:

In a small saucepan, heat the heavy cream over medium heat until it just begins to simmer.
Remove from heat and add the semisweet chocolate chips. Let it sit for a minute, then stir until smooth and glossy.
Pour the chocolate ganache over the cooled brownies and spread it evenly.
Allow the ganache to set before cutting the brownies into squares.
Serve and enjoy the decadent Triple Chocolate Brownies!

These brownies are a chocolate lover's dream with three layers of chocolatey goodness. Feel free to customize them by adding nuts or additional chocolate varieties. Include any serving suggestions or storage tips in your cookbook. Enjoy!

**Chocolate Banana Bread**

*Ingredients:*

- 3 ripe bananas, mashed
- 1/2 cup unsalted butter, melted
- 1 teaspoon vanilla extract
- 2 large eggs
- 1 cup granulated sugar
- 1 3/4 cups all-purpose flour
- 1/4 cup unsweetened cocoa powder
- 1 teaspoon baking soda
- 1/4 teaspoon salt
- 1 cup semisweet chocolate chips

*Instructions:*

Preheat your oven to 350°F (175°C). Grease a 9x5-inch loaf pan.
In a large mixing bowl, mash the ripe bananas with a fork or potato masher.
Add melted butter to the mashed bananas and mix well.
Stir in the vanilla extract and eggs until the mixture is well combined.
In a separate bowl, whisk together the sugar, flour, cocoa powder, baking soda, and salt.
Gradually add the dry ingredients to the banana mixture, stirring until just combined.
Fold in the semisweet chocolate chips.
Pour the batter into the greased loaf pan, spreading it evenly.
Bake in the preheated oven for 60-70 minutes or until a toothpick inserted into the center comes out with a few moist crumbs (not wet batter).
Allow the chocolate banana bread to cool in the pan for about 10 minutes before transferring it to a wire rack to cool completely.
Once cooled, slice and serve. Enjoy the moist and chocolatey goodness!

This Chocolate Banana Bread is a delightful twist on the classic banana bread, combining the rich flavor of chocolate with the sweetness of ripe bananas. Feel free to customize by adding nuts or additional chocolate chunks. Include any tips for achieving the perfect texture in your cookbook. Enjoy!

**Chocolate Dipped Pretzels**

*Ingredients:*

- Pretzel rods or twists
- 8 oz (about 1 1/3 cups) semisweet or dark chocolate, chopped
- White chocolate for drizzling (optional)
- Toppings (optional): crushed nuts, sprinkles, coconut flakes

*Instructions:*

Line a baking sheet with parchment paper.

In a heatproof bowl, melt the semisweet or dark chocolate. Use a double boiler or melt in the microwave in short bursts, stirring frequently until smooth.

Dip each pretzel rod or twist into the melted chocolate, coating it about two-thirds of the way up. Allow excess chocolate to drip back into the bowl.

Place the chocolate-dipped pretzels on the prepared baking sheet.

If desired, melt white chocolate and drizzle it over the dipped pretzels for a decorative touch.

While the chocolate is still wet, you can sprinkle the pretzels with your choice of toppings such as crushed nuts, sprinkles, or coconut flakes.

Allow the chocolate-dipped pretzels to set at room temperature or, for faster setting, place them in the refrigerator for about 30 minutes.

Once the chocolate is fully set, transfer the pretzels to a serving plate.

Serve and enjoy these sweet and salty Chocolate Dipped Pretzels as a delightful snack or party treat.

Feel free to get creative with the toppings or even use different types of chocolate for dipping. Include any tips for achieving the perfect chocolate coating and presentation in your cookbook. These Chocolate Dipped Pretzels make for a delicious and visually appealing treat!

**Nutella Chocolate Milkshake**

*Ingredients:*

- 2 cups chocolate ice cream
- 1/2 cup milk
- 1/3 cup Nutella
- 2 tablespoons chocolate syrup
- Whipped cream for topping
- Chocolate shavings or chopped hazelnuts for garnish (optional)

*Instructions:*

In a blender, combine chocolate ice cream, milk, Nutella, and chocolate syrup.
Blend the ingredients until smooth and creamy. If the milkshake is too thick, you can add a bit more milk and blend again.
Pour the Nutella chocolate milkshake into tall glasses.
Top each milkshake with a generous dollop of whipped cream.
If desired, garnish with chocolate shavings or chopped hazelnuts for added texture and flavor.
Serve immediately and enjoy this indulgent Nutella Chocolate Milkshake!

Feel free to adjust the quantities of Nutella and chocolate syrup based on your preference for sweetness. You can also add a scoop of vanilla ice cream for an extra creamy texture. Include any tips for achieving the perfect consistency in your cookbook. This Nutella Chocolate Milkshake is a delightful treat for Nutella lovers and chocolate enthusiasts alike!

**Mint Chocolate Chip Ice Cream**

*Ingredients:*

- 2 cups heavy cream
- 1 cup whole milk
- 3/4 cup granulated sugar
- 1 teaspoon pure peppermint extract
- 1/2 teaspoon pure vanilla extract
- Green food coloring (optional, for color)
- 1 cup chocolate chips or chocolate chunks

*Instructions:*

In a mixing bowl, whisk together heavy cream, whole milk, and granulated sugar until the sugar is completely dissolved.
Stir in the peppermint extract and vanilla extract. If desired, add a few drops of green food coloring to achieve the classic mint color.
Chill the mixture in the refrigerator for at least 2 hours or overnight.
Once chilled, pour the mixture into an ice cream maker and churn according to the manufacturer's instructions.
During the last few minutes of churning, add the chocolate chips or chocolate chunks to evenly distribute them throughout the ice cream.
Transfer the churned ice cream to a lidded container and freeze for at least 4 hours or until firm.
Scoop and serve the Mint Chocolate Chip Ice Cream in bowls or cones.
Garnish with additional chocolate chips or mint leaves if desired.
Enjoy the cool and refreshing Mint Chocolate Chip Ice Cream!

Feel free to customize the level of mint flavor and sweetness according to your taste preferences. You can also experiment with different types of chocolate, such as dark chocolate or mint chocolate, for an extra twist. Include any tips for achieving a creamy texture in your cookbook. This homemade Mint Chocolate Chip Ice Cream is perfect for cooling down on a warm day!

**Chocolate Pots de Crème**

*Ingredients:*

- 6 oz (about 1 cup) bittersweet or semisweet chocolate, finely chopped
- 2 cups heavy cream
- 1/2 cup whole milk
- 1/2 cup granulated sugar
- 6 large egg yolks
- 1 teaspoon pure vanilla extract
- Pinch of salt
- Whipped cream and chocolate shavings for garnish (optional)

*Instructions:*

Preheat your oven to 325°F (163°C). Place six ramekins or small jars in a baking dish.
In a heatproof bowl, place the finely chopped chocolate.
In a saucepan, heat the heavy cream, whole milk, and granulated sugar over medium heat. Stir occasionally until the mixture is hot but not boiling.
Pour the hot cream mixture over the chopped chocolate. Let it sit for a minute, then stir until the chocolate is completely melted and the mixture is smooth.
In a separate bowl, whisk together the egg yolks, vanilla extract, and a pinch of salt.
Slowly pour the chocolate mixture into the egg yolk mixture, whisking constantly to avoid curdling.
Strain the custard through a fine-mesh sieve into a bowl to ensure a smooth texture.
Divide the custard among the ramekins or jars in the baking dish.
Fill the baking dish with hot water to come halfway up the sides of the ramekins, creating a water bath.
Cover the baking dish with aluminum foil and bake in the preheated oven for 35-40 minutes or until the edges are set but the center is still slightly jiggly.
Remove from the oven and let the pots de crème cool in the water bath. Once cooled, transfer to the refrigerator to chill for at least 4 hours or overnight.
Before serving, garnish with a dollop of whipped cream and chocolate shavings if desired.
Enjoy the velvety and luxurious Chocolate Pots de Crème!

Include any tips for achieving a silky smooth texture and the importance of the water bath in your cookbook. This classic French dessert is sure to impress with its rich chocolate flavor and creamy consistency.

**Chocolate Covered Nuts**

*Ingredients:*

- 2 cups mixed nuts (almonds, cashews, walnuts, etc.)
- 8 oz (about 1 1/3 cups) semisweet or dark chocolate, chopped
- 1 tablespoon coconut oil (optional, for smoother chocolate)
- Sea salt for sprinkling (optional)

*Instructions:*

Line a baking sheet with parchment paper.

In a heatproof bowl, melt the semisweet or dark chocolate. You can use a double boiler or melt in the microwave in short bursts, stirring frequently until smooth. If desired, add coconut oil to the melted chocolate for a smoother consistency.

Add the mixed nuts to the melted chocolate and stir until all the nuts are evenly coated.

Using a fork or a chocolate dipping tool, lift each chocolate-covered nut, allowing excess chocolate to drip back into the bowl, and place it on the prepared baking sheet.

If desired, sprinkle a bit of sea salt over the chocolate-covered nuts for a sweet and salty combination.

Allow the chocolate-covered nuts to set at room temperature or, for faster setting, place them in the refrigerator for about 30 minutes.

Once the chocolate is fully set, transfer the chocolate-covered nuts to an airtight container.

Store in a cool place or refrigerate until ready to serve.

Enjoy these delicious Chocolate Covered Nuts as a snack or a sweet treat!

Feel free to customize the recipe by using your favorite combination of nuts or adding a sprinkle of your preferred spices. Include any tips for achieving perfectly coated nuts and storage suggestions in your cookbook. These chocolate-covered nuts are a delightful and satisfying snack for any occasion!

**Chocolate Tiramisu**

*Ingredients:*

For the Chocolate Mascarpone Filling:

- 1 1/2 cups heavy cream
- 8 oz mascarpone cheese, softened
- 1 cup powdered sugar
- 1 teaspoon vanilla extract
- 1/2 cup unsweetened cocoa powder
- 1/2 cup chocolate chips or chopped chocolate

For the Coffee Soaking Liquid:

- 1 1/2 cups strong brewed coffee, cooled to room temperature
- 2 tablespoons coffee liqueur (optional)
- 1 tablespoon sugar (optional)

Other Ingredients:

- Ladyfinger cookies (about 24)
- Cocoa powder for dusting

*Instructions:*

For the Chocolate Mascarpone Filling:

In a mixing bowl, whip the heavy cream until stiff peaks form.
In another bowl, beat the mascarpone cheese, powdered sugar, and vanilla extract until smooth.
Gently fold the whipped cream into the mascarpone mixture until well combined.
Fold in the unsweetened cocoa powder and chocolate chips or chopped chocolate.

For the Coffee Soaking Liquid:

In a shallow dish, combine the brewed coffee, coffee liqueur (if using), and sugar (if desired). Mix until sugar is dissolved.

Assembling the Chocolate Tiramisu:

Dip each ladyfinger into the coffee soaking liquid for a few seconds, ensuring they are moistened but not soaked.
Arrange a layer of dipped ladyfingers in the bottom of a serving dish or individual glasses.
Spread half of the chocolate mascarpone filling over the ladyfingers layer.
Repeat the process with another layer of dipped ladyfingers and the remaining chocolate mascarpone filling.
Refrigerate the chocolate tiramisu for at least 4 hours or overnight to allow the flavors to meld and the dessert to set.
Before serving, dust the top with cocoa powder.
Serve chilled and enjoy the rich and chocolaty goodness of Chocolate Tiramisu!

Feel free to customize the recipe by adjusting the sweetness or adding more chocolate layers. Include any tips for assembling the tiramisu and achieving a perfect balance of flavors in your cookbook. This chocolate twist on the classic Italian dessert is sure to be a hit!

**Chocolate Zucchini Bread**

*Ingredients:*

- 2 cups grated zucchini (about 2 medium zucchinis)
- 1 1/2 cups all-purpose flour
- 1/2 cup unsweetened cocoa powder
- 1 teaspoon baking soda
- 1/2 teaspoon baking powder
- 1/2 teaspoon salt
- 1/2 cup unsalted butter, melted
- 1/2 cup vegetable oil
- 1 cup granulated sugar
- 1/2 cup brown sugar, packed
- 3 large eggs
- 2 teaspoons vanilla extract
- 1 cup semisweet chocolate chips

*Instructions:*

Preheat your oven to 350°F (175°C). Grease and flour a 9x5-inch loaf pan.

Grate the zucchinis and set aside. If the zucchini is very watery, you can squeeze out excess moisture with a paper towel.

In a large bowl, whisk together the flour, cocoa powder, baking soda, baking powder, and salt.

In another bowl, whisk together the melted butter, vegetable oil, granulated sugar, brown sugar, eggs, and vanilla extract until well combined.

Add the grated zucchini to the wet ingredients and stir until evenly distributed.

Gradually add the dry ingredients to the wet ingredients, stirring until just combined.

Fold in the semisweet chocolate chips.

Pour the batter into the prepared loaf pan, spreading it evenly.

Bake in the preheated oven for 55-65 minutes or until a toothpick inserted into the center comes out with a few moist crumbs.

Allow the chocolate zucchini bread to cool in the pan for about 10 minutes before transferring it to a wire rack to cool completely.

Once cooled, slice and enjoy this moist and chocolaty Chocolate Zucchini Bread!

Feel free to customize the recipe by adding chopped nuts or a swirl of chocolate ganache. Include any tips for achieving the perfect texture and moistness in your cookbook. This chocolate zucchini bread is a wonderful way to incorporate veggies into a sweet treat!

**Mexican Hot Chocolate**

*Ingredients:*

- 4 cups whole milk
- 4 oz bittersweet or semisweet chocolate, finely chopped
- 2 tablespoons cocoa powder
- 1/4 cup granulated sugar (adjust to taste)
- 1 teaspoon ground cinnamon
- 1/4 teaspoon chili powder (optional, for a hint of spice)
- 1 teaspoon vanilla extract
- Pinch of salt
- Whipped cream, cinnamon sticks, or chocolate shavings for garnish (optional)

*Instructions:*

In a saucepan over medium heat, warm the milk until it begins to simmer. Do not boil.
Add the finely chopped chocolate, cocoa powder, sugar, ground cinnamon, and chili powder (if using) to the simmering milk.
Whisk the mixture continuously until the chocolate is completely melted and the ingredients are well combined.
Once the chocolate mixture is smooth, add the vanilla extract and a pinch of salt. Continue to whisk.
Taste the hot chocolate and adjust the sweetness by adding more sugar if needed.
Continue to heat the Mexican hot chocolate until it is hot but not boiling, stirring occasionally.
Remove the saucepan from heat and pour the Mexican hot chocolate into mugs.
If desired, garnish with a dollop of whipped cream, a cinnamon stick, or chocolate shavings.
Serve immediately and enjoy the rich and flavorful Mexican Hot Chocolate!

Feel free to customize the spice level by adjusting the amount of chili powder, and don't forget to include any personal tips or variations in your cookbook. This Mexican Hot Chocolate is a comforting and indulgent treat with a delightful blend of chocolate and warm spices.

**Chocolate Covered Oreos**

*Ingredients:*

- 1 package of Oreo cookies (about 24 cookies)
- 8 oz (about 1 1/3 cups) semisweet or dark chocolate, chopped
- White chocolate for drizzling (optional)
- Sprinkles, crushed nuts, or other toppings for decoration (optional)

*Instructions:*

Line a baking sheet with parchment paper.

In a heatproof bowl, melt the semisweet or dark chocolate. You can use a double boiler or melt in the microwave in short bursts, stirring frequently until smooth.

Dip each Oreo cookie into the melted chocolate, ensuring it is fully coated. Use a fork or dipping tool to lift the cookie, allowing excess chocolate to drip back into the bowl.

Place the chocolate-covered Oreos on the prepared baking sheet.

If desired, melt white chocolate and drizzle it over the chocolate-covered Oreos for a decorative touch.

While the chocolate is still wet, you can sprinkle the Oreos with your choice of toppings such as sprinkles or crushed nuts.

Allow the chocolate-covered Oreos to set at room temperature or, for faster setting, place them in the refrigerator for about 30 minutes.

Once the chocolate is fully set, transfer the Chocolate Covered Oreos to a serving plate.

Serve and enjoy these delightful treats as a sweet snack or party dessert!

Feel free to get creative with the toppings or even use different types of chocolate for dipping. Include any tips for achieving the perfect chocolate coating and presentation in your cookbook. These Chocolate Covered Oreos are a fun and delicious treat for any occasion!

**Chocolate Soufflé**

*Ingredients:*

- 4 oz bittersweet chocolate, finely chopped
- 3 tablespoons unsalted butter
- 1/4 cup all-purpose flour
- 1/4 cup cocoa powder
- 1 cup whole milk
- 4 large egg yolks
- 1 teaspoon vanilla extract
- Pinch of salt
- 5 large egg whites
- 1/4 cup granulated sugar
- Powdered sugar for dusting

*Instructions:*

Preheat your oven to 375°F (190°C). Butter and sugar the insides of four 6-ounce ramekins or soufflé dishes.

In a heatproof bowl set over simmering water, melt the finely chopped bittersweet chocolate and butter together. Stir until smooth, then remove from heat.

In a separate saucepan, whisk together the flour, cocoa powder, and milk over medium heat. Continue whisking until the mixture thickens to form a smooth chocolate sauce.

Remove the saucepan from heat and gradually whisk the chocolate sauce into the melted chocolate and butter mixture. Stir in the egg yolks and vanilla extract. Add a pinch of salt and mix until well combined. Set aside.

In a clean, dry bowl, use an electric mixer to whip the egg whites until foamy. Gradually add the granulated sugar and continue whipping until stiff peaks form.

Gently fold one-third of the whipped egg whites into the chocolate mixture to lighten it. Then, carefully fold in the remaining egg whites until no white streaks remain.

Divide the soufflé batter evenly among the prepared ramekins, filling them almost to the top.

Run your thumb around the edge of each ramekin to create a slight indentation. Place the ramekins on a baking sheet and bake in the preheated oven for 15-18 minutes, or until the soufflés have risen and set with a slightly gooey center.

Dust the tops of the soufflés with powdered sugar and serve immediately. Enjoy the decadence of Chocolate Soufflé straight from the oven!

Include any tips for achieving the perfect rise and texture in your cookbook. This Chocolate Soufflé is a classic and elegant dessert that's sure to impress.

**Chocolate Coconut Macaroons**

*Ingredients:*

- 3 cups shredded coconut (sweetened)
- 3/4 cup sweetened condensed milk
- 2 teaspoons vanilla extract
- 1/4 teaspoon salt
- 2 large egg whites
- 1 cup semisweet or dark chocolate chips
- 1 tablespoon coconut oil (optional, for smoother chocolate)

*Instructions:*

Preheat your oven to 325°F (163°C). Line a baking sheet with parchment paper.
In a large bowl, combine the shredded coconut, sweetened condensed milk, vanilla extract, and salt. Mix until well combined.
In a separate bowl, beat the egg whites until stiff peaks form.
Gently fold the beaten egg whites into the coconut mixture until evenly combined.
Using a spoon or cookie scoop, drop rounded mounds of the coconut mixture onto the prepared baking sheet.
Bake in the preheated oven for 15-18 minutes or until the edges of the macaroons are golden brown.
Allow the macaroons to cool completely on the baking sheet.
In a heatproof bowl, melt the chocolate chips. You can use a double boiler or melt in the microwave in short bursts, stirring frequently until smooth. Add coconut oil for a smoother chocolate consistency if desired.
Dip the bottom of each cooled macaroon into the melted chocolate, allowing excess chocolate to drip back into the bowl.
Place the chocolate-dipped macaroons on parchment paper to let the chocolate set.
If desired, drizzle additional chocolate over the top of the macaroons for decoration.
Allow the chocolate to set completely before serving or storing.
Enjoy these delicious Chocolate Coconut Macaroons as a sweet treat!

Feel free to get creative with the chocolate drizzle or even add chopped nuts for extra crunch. Include any tips for achieving the perfect texture and presentation in your cookbook. These Chocolate Coconut Macaroons are a delightful combination of chewy coconut and rich chocolate.

**Chocolate Espresso Martini**

*Ingredients:*

- 1 1/2 oz vodka
- 1 oz coffee liqueur (such as Kahlúa)
- 1 oz freshly brewed espresso, cooled
- 1/2 oz chocolate liqueur
- Ice cubes
- Chocolate shavings or coffee beans for garnish (optional)

*Instructions:*

Brew a shot of espresso and let it cool to room temperature.
Fill a cocktail shaker with ice cubes.
Add vodka, coffee liqueur, cooled espresso, and chocolate liqueur to the shaker.
Shake the mixture vigorously for about 15-20 seconds to chill and combine the ingredients.
Strain the mixture into a chilled martini glass.
If desired, garnish the Chocolate Espresso Martini with chocolate shavings or coffee beans.
Serve immediately and enjoy the rich and caffeinated flavors!

Feel free to adjust the ratios to suit your taste preferences, and don't forget to include any personal tips or variations in your cookbook. This Chocolate Espresso Martini is a perfect after-dinner drink for coffee and chocolate enthusiasts!

## Chocolate Covered Caramel Apples

*Ingredients:*

- 4 medium-sized apples (Granny Smith or your preferred variety)
- 1 package (about 11 oz) soft caramel candies
- 2 tablespoons heavy cream
- 8 oz (about 1 1/3 cups) semisweet or dark chocolate, chopped
- Toppings (optional): chopped nuts, sprinkles, shredded coconut

*Instructions:*

Wash and thoroughly dry the apples. Remove the stems and insert a sturdy wooden stick or popsicle stick into the top of each apple, pushing it about halfway through.

Line a baking sheet with parchment paper.

Unwrap the caramel candies and place them in a microwave-safe bowl. Add the heavy cream.

Microwave the caramel and cream mixture in 30-second intervals, stirring each time, until the caramel is completely melted and smooth.

Dip each apple into the melted caramel, rotating it to ensure even coating. Allow excess caramel to drip back into the bowl.

Place the caramel-coated apples on the prepared baking sheet and let them cool until the caramel is set.

In a heatproof bowl, melt the semisweet or dark chocolate. You can use a double boiler or melt in the microwave in short bursts, stirring frequently until smooth.

Dip each caramel-coated apple into the melted chocolate, coating it about two-thirds of the way up. Allow excess chocolate to drip back into the bowl.

If desired, roll the chocolate-covered apples in chopped nuts, sprinkles, or shredded coconut while the chocolate is still wet.

Place the chocolate-covered caramel apples back on the parchment-lined baking sheet.

Allow the chocolate to set at room temperature or, for faster setting, place the apples in the refrigerator for about 30 minutes.

Once the chocolate is fully set, transfer the Chocolate Covered Caramel Apples to a serving plate.

Serve and enjoy these delightful treats as a decadent dessert or a festive treat!

Feel free to get creative with the toppings or even drizzle additional chocolate over the apples for decoration. Include any tips for achieving the perfect caramel and chocolate coating in your cookbook. These Chocolate Covered Caramel Apples are a wonderful combination of sweet, chewy caramel and rich chocolate!

**Chocolate Fondue**

*Ingredients:*

- 8 oz (about 1 1/3 cups) semisweet or dark chocolate, finely chopped
- 1 cup heavy cream
- 2 tablespoons unsalted butter
- 1 teaspoon vanilla extract
- Pinch of salt
- Assorted dippables: strawberries, banana slices, pineapple chunks, marshmallows, pretzels, cubes of pound cake, etc.

*Instructions:*

In a saucepan over medium heat, bring the heavy cream to a gentle simmer. Do not boil.
Place the finely chopped chocolate in a heatproof bowl.
Pour the hot cream over the chocolate. Let it sit for a minute, then stir until the chocolate is completely melted and the mixture is smooth.
Add unsalted butter, vanilla extract, and a pinch of salt to the melted chocolate mixture. Stir until the butter is melted and the ingredients are well combined.
Transfer the chocolate fondue to a fondue pot or a heatproof serving bowl.
Set up your favorite dippables on a serving platter.
Light the fondue pot if using, and keep the chocolate warm over a low flame.
Invite guests to dip their favorite treats into the chocolate fondue using fondue forks or skewers.
Enjoy the delightful experience of Chocolate Fondue!

Feel free to customize the dippables based on your preferences. Include any tips for maintaining the ideal consistency of the fondue and suggestions for creative dippables in your cookbook. Chocolate Fondue is a fun and interactive dessert that's perfect for parties and gatherings!

**Chocolate Pecan Pie**

*Ingredients:*

For the Pie Crust:

- 1 1/4 cups all-purpose flour
- 1/2 cup unsalted butter, cold and cut into small cubes
- 1/4 cup granulated sugar
- 1/4 teaspoon salt
- 2-3 tablespoons ice water

For the Filling:

- 1 cup granulated sugar
- 1 cup light corn syrup
- 1/3 cup unsalted butter, melted
- 4 large eggs, beaten
- 1 teaspoon vanilla extract
- 1/4 teaspoon salt
- 1 1/2 cups pecan halves
- 1 cup semisweet chocolate chips

*Instructions:*

For the Pie Crust:

In a food processor, combine the flour, sugar, and salt. Add the cold butter cubes and pulse until the mixture resembles coarse crumbs.
With the processor running, gradually add the ice water until the dough comes together. Be careful not to overmix.
Turn the dough out onto a lightly floured surface and shape it into a disk. Wrap in plastic wrap and refrigerate for at least 1 hour.
Preheat your oven to 350°F (175°C).
Roll out the chilled pie dough on a floured surface and fit it into a 9-inch pie dish. Trim any excess and crimp the edges.

For the Filling:

In a mixing bowl, whisk together sugar, corn syrup, melted butter, beaten eggs, vanilla extract, and salt until well combined.
Sprinkle pecan halves and chocolate chips evenly over the pie crust.
Pour the filling mixture over the pecans and chocolate chips.
Bake in the preheated oven for 50-60 minutes or until the filling is set. If the crust edges start to brown too quickly, cover them with aluminum foil.
Allow the Chocolate Pecan Pie to cool completely before slicing.
Serve and enjoy this rich and indulgent dessert!

Feel free to customize the pie by adding a scoop of vanilla ice cream or a dollop of whipped cream when serving. Include any tips for achieving the perfect crust and filling consistency in your cookbook. This Chocolate Pecan Pie is a delightful twist on the classic pecan pie!

**Chocolate Hazelnut Biscotti**

*Ingredients:*

- 2 cups all-purpose flour
- 1/2 cup unsweetened cocoa powder
- 1 teaspoon baking soda
- 1/4 teaspoon salt
- 1/2 cup unsalted butter, softened
- 1 cup granulated sugar
- 2 large eggs
- 1 teaspoon vanilla extract
- 1 cup hazelnuts, toasted and chopped
- 1 cup semisweet chocolate chips or chunks

*Instructions:*

Preheat your oven to 350°F (175°C). Line a baking sheet with parchment paper.
In a medium bowl, whisk together the flour, cocoa powder, baking soda, and salt.
In a large bowl, cream together the softened butter and granulated sugar until light and fluffy.
Beat in the eggs, one at a time, and then add the vanilla extract. Mix until well combined.
Gradually add the dry ingredients to the wet ingredients, mixing until a dough forms.
Fold in the toasted and chopped hazelnuts, as well as the semisweet chocolate chips or chunks.
Divide the dough in half. On the prepared baking sheet, shape each portion into a log about 12 inches long and 2 inches wide, spacing them apart.
Bake in the preheated oven for 25-30 minutes or until the logs are set. They will still be slightly soft in the center.
Remove from the oven and let the logs cool on the baking sheet for about 10 minutes.
Reduce the oven temperature to 325°F (163°C).
Transfer the logs to a cutting board and slice diagonally into 1/2-inch slices.
Place the sliced biscotti back on the baking sheet, cut side down.
Bake for an additional 10-12 minutes or until the biscotti are crisp and firm.
Allow the Chocolate Hazelnut Biscotti to cool completely before serving.
Enjoy these delightful biscotti with a cup of coffee or your favorite hot beverage!

Include any tips for achieving the perfect crispness and flavor in your cookbook. These Chocolate Hazelnut Biscotti are a perfect combination of rich chocolate, toasted hazelnuts, and a satisfying crunch!

**Chocolate Avocado Mousse**

*Ingredients:*

- 2 ripe avocados, peeled and pitted
- 1/2 cup unsweetened cocoa powder
- 1/2 cup maple syrup or honey
- 1/3 cup coconut milk or almond milk
- 1 teaspoon vanilla extract
- Pinch of salt
- Fresh berries or chopped nuts for garnish (optional)

*Instructions:*

In a food processor or blender, combine the ripe avocados, cocoa powder, maple syrup or honey, coconut milk or almond milk, vanilla extract, and a pinch of salt. Blend the ingredients until smooth and creamy. Stop and scrape down the sides of the blender or food processor as needed.

Taste the chocolate avocado mixture and adjust the sweetness or cocoa level if desired.

Once the mixture is smooth and well combined, transfer the Chocolate Avocado Mousse to serving glasses or bowls.

Refrigerate the mousse for at least 1-2 hours to chill and allow the flavors to meld.

Before serving, garnish with fresh berries or chopped nuts if desired.

Enjoy this rich and creamy Chocolate Avocado Mousse as a healthy and indulgent dessert!

Feel free to experiment with toppings or add a sprinkle of sea salt for a sweet and salty contrast. Include any tips for achieving the perfect consistency and flavor in your cookbook. This Chocolate Avocado Mousse is a guilt-free treat that's both satisfying and nutritious!

**Chocolate Raspberry Tart**

*Ingredients:*

For the Chocolate Tart Shell:

- 1 1/4 cups all-purpose flour
- 1/4 cup unsweetened cocoa powder
- 1/2 cup unsalted butter, cold and cut into small pieces
- 1/4 cup granulated sugar
- 1 large egg yolk
- 2 tablespoons ice water

For the Chocolate Ganache Filling:

- 8 oz semisweet or dark chocolate, finely chopped
- 1 cup heavy cream
- 2 tablespoons unsalted butter
- 1 teaspoon vanilla extract

For the Raspberry Topping:

- 2 cups fresh raspberries
- 2 tablespoons raspberry jam, melted

*Instructions:*

For the Chocolate Tart Shell:

> In a food processor, combine the flour, cocoa powder, cold butter pieces, and granulated sugar. Pulse until the mixture resembles coarse crumbs.
> Add the egg yolk and ice water, and pulse until the dough comes together. Be careful not to overmix.
> Turn the dough out onto a lightly floured surface, shape it into a disk, wrap in plastic wrap, and refrigerate for at least 30 minutes.
> Preheat your oven to 375°F (190°C).
> Roll out the chilled dough on a floured surface and fit it into a tart pan. Trim any excess and prick the bottom with a fork.
> Line the tart shell with parchment paper and fill with pie weights or dried beans.

Bake in the preheated oven for about 15 minutes. Remove the weights and parchment paper, then bake for an additional 10-12 minutes or until the crust is set and slightly golden. Allow it to cool.

For the Chocolate Ganache Filling:

Place the finely chopped chocolate in a heatproof bowl.
In a saucepan, heat the heavy cream and butter over medium heat until it just begins to simmer.
Pour the hot cream mixture over the chocolate. Let it sit for a minute, then stir until the chocolate is completely melted and the mixture is smooth.
Stir in the vanilla extract. Pour the chocolate ganache into the cooled tart shell.
Refrigerate the tart for at least 2 hours or until the ganache is set.

For the Raspberry Topping:

Arrange fresh raspberries on top of the chilled chocolate ganache.
Brush melted raspberry jam over the raspberries for a shiny glaze.
Refrigerate the tart until ready to serve.
Slice and enjoy this elegant Chocolate Raspberry Tart!

Include any tips for achieving the perfect tart crust and glossy raspberry topping in your cookbook. This Chocolate Raspberry Tart is a decadent combination of rich chocolate and vibrant raspberries!

**White Chocolate Macadamia Nut Cookies**

*Ingredients:*

- 1 cup unsalted butter, softened
- 1 cup granulated sugar
- 1 cup packed light brown sugar
- 2 large eggs
- 1 teaspoon vanilla extract
- 3 cups all-purpose flour
- 1 teaspoon baking soda
- 1/2 teaspoon baking powder
- 1/2 teaspoon salt
- 1 1/2 cups white chocolate chips or chunks
- 1 1/2 cups macadamia nuts, chopped

*Instructions:*

Preheat your oven to 350°F (175°C). Line baking sheets with parchment paper.
In a large bowl, cream together the softened butter, granulated sugar, and brown sugar until light and fluffy.
Add the eggs one at a time, beating well after each addition. Stir in the vanilla extract.
In a separate bowl, whisk together the flour, baking soda, baking powder, and salt.
Gradually add the dry ingredients to the wet ingredients, mixing until just combined.
Fold in the white chocolate chips or chunks and chopped macadamia nuts.
Drop rounded tablespoons of cookie dough onto the prepared baking sheets, spacing them about 2 inches apart.
Bake in the preheated oven for 10-12 minutes or until the edges are golden but the centers are still soft.
Allow the cookies to cool on the baking sheets for a few minutes before transferring them to a wire rack to cool completely.
Enjoy these delicious White Chocolate Macadamia Nut Cookies with a glass of milk or your favorite beverage!

Feel free to customize the recipe by adding a sprinkle of sea salt on top of the cookies or using different types of white chocolate. Include any tips for achieving the perfect balance of chewiness and crunch in your cookbook. These cookies are a classic combination of sweet white chocolate and rich macadamia nuts!

**Chocolate Peanut Butter Cups**

*Ingredients:*

- 1 cup semisweet or dark chocolate chips
- 1 tablespoon coconut oil or unsalted butter
- 1/2 cup creamy peanut butter
- 3 tablespoons powdered sugar
- 1/2 teaspoon vanilla extract
- Pinch of salt

*Instructions:*

Line a mini muffin tin with paper or silicone cupcake liners.
In a microwave-safe bowl, combine the chocolate chips and coconut oil or butter. Microwave in 30-second intervals, stirring between each, until the chocolate is completely melted and smooth.
Spoon a small amount of melted chocolate into the bottom of each cupcake liner, spreading it to cover the bottom.
Place the muffin tin in the freezer for about 10 minutes to allow the chocolate to set.
In another bowl, mix together peanut butter, powdered sugar, vanilla extract, and a pinch of salt until well combined.
Remove the muffin tin from the freezer and place a small dollop of the peanut butter mixture on top of the set chocolate in each cup.
Flatten the peanut butter slightly with the back of a spoon.
Pour the remaining melted chocolate over the peanut butter, ensuring it covers and seals the peanut butter filling.
Return the muffin tin to the freezer for another 10-15 minutes to set the chocolate.
Once set, remove the Chocolate Peanut Butter Cups from the muffin tin.
Peel off the cupcake liners and serve the delightful treats!

Feel free to experiment by using different types of chocolate or adding toppings like chopped nuts or sea salt. Include any tips for achieving the perfect chocolate-to-peanut butter ratio in your cookbook. These homemade Chocolate Peanut Butter Cups are a classic and irresistible treat!

**Dark Chocolate Almond Bark**

*Ingredients:*

- 12 oz dark chocolate (70% cocoa or your preferred percentage), finely chopped
- 1 cup whole almonds, toasted
- Sea salt for sprinkling (optional)
- 1/2 teaspoon vanilla extract (optional)

*Instructions:*

Line a baking sheet with parchment paper or a silicone baking mat.
In a heatproof bowl, melt the dark chocolate using a double boiler or by microwaving in short intervals, stirring each time until smooth.
If using, stir in the vanilla extract into the melted chocolate.
Once the chocolate is fully melted and smooth, fold in the toasted almonds until they are evenly coated.
Pour the chocolate and almond mixture onto the prepared baking sheet, spreading it out into an even layer.
If desired, sprinkle a pinch of sea salt over the top for a sweet and salty flavor.
Place the baking sheet in the refrigerator for about 1 hour or until the chocolate is completely set.
Once set, break the Dark Chocolate Almond Bark into smaller pieces.
Store in an airtight container in a cool place or the refrigerator.
Enjoy this delightful Dark Chocolate Almond Bark as a snack or a homemade gift!

Feel free to customize the recipe by adding dried fruits, other nuts, or even a drizzle of white chocolate. Include any tips for achieving the perfect smoothness and flavor in your cookbook. Dark Chocolate Almond Bark is a simple and elegant treat that's perfect for sharing!

**Chocolate Pudding**

*Ingredients:*

- 1/2 cup granulated sugar
- 1/4 cup unsweetened cocoa powder
- 1/4 cup cornstarch
- Pinch of salt
- 2 3/4 cups whole milk
- 4 oz semisweet or dark chocolate, finely chopped
- 2 teaspoons vanilla extract
- Whipped cream for garnish (optional)

*Instructions:*

In a medium-sized saucepan, whisk together the sugar, cocoa powder, cornstarch, and a pinch of salt.
Gradually whisk in the whole milk until the mixture is smooth and well combined.
Place the saucepan over medium heat and bring the mixture to a gentle boil, stirring constantly.
Once the mixture begins to boil, reduce the heat to low and continue to stir for 1-2 minutes until it thickens.
Remove the saucepan from heat and add the finely chopped chocolate. Stir until the chocolate is fully melted and the pudding is smooth.
Stir in the vanilla extract.
Pour the chocolate pudding into serving dishes or into a large bowl if serving family-style.
Allow the pudding to cool slightly at room temperature, then refrigerate for at least 2 hours or until chilled and set.
Before serving, you can top the chocolate pudding with a dollop of whipped cream if desired.
Serve and enjoy this rich and creamy Chocolate Pudding!

Feel free to customize the recipe by adding a sprinkle of chocolate shavings or crushed nuts on top. Include any tips for achieving the perfect consistency and flavor in your cookbook. This Chocolate Pudding is a comforting and timeless dessert that's sure to be a hit!

**Chocolate Orange Trifle**

*Ingredients:*

For the Chocolate Cake Layer:

- 1 box (about 16 oz) chocolate cake mix (plus ingredients needed for preparation)

For the Orange Custard Layer:

- 2 cups whole milk
- 1 cup granulated sugar
- 1/2 cup cornstarch
- Pinch of salt
- 4 large egg yolks
- Zest of 2 oranges
- 1/2 cup fresh orange juice
- 2 tablespoons unsalted butter
- 1 teaspoon vanilla extract

For the Chocolate Ganache Layer:

- 8 oz semisweet or dark chocolate, finely chopped
- 1 cup heavy cream
- Zest of 1 orange (for garnish)
- Chocolate shavings (for garnish)

*Instructions:*

For the Chocolate Cake Layer:

> Prepare the chocolate cake according to the package instructions. Allow it to cool completely.
> Once cooled, cut the chocolate cake into cubes.

For the Orange Custard Layer:

In a medium saucepan, whisk together the sugar, cornstarch, and a pinch of salt.
In a separate bowl, whisk together the milk and egg yolks.
Gradually whisk the milk mixture into the sugar mixture until smooth.
Place the saucepan over medium heat and cook, stirring constantly, until the mixture thickens.
Remove from heat and stir in the orange zest, orange juice, butter, and vanilla extract.
Allow the custard to cool to room temperature.

For the Chocolate Ganache Layer:

In a heatproof bowl, combine the finely chopped chocolate and heavy cream.
Heat the mixture in the microwave or using a double boiler, stirring until the chocolate is completely melted and smooth.

Assembling the Trifle:

In a trifle dish or individual serving glasses, layer the chocolate cake cubes, followed by the orange custard, and then the chocolate ganache.
Repeat the layers until the trifle dish is filled, finishing with a layer of chocolate ganache on top.
Garnish the top with orange zest and chocolate shavings.
Refrigerate the Chocolate Orange Trifle for at least 4 hours or overnight to allow the flavors to meld.
Serve and enjoy this decadent and citrusy dessert!

Include any tips for achieving beautiful layers and presentation in your cookbook. This Chocolate Orange Trifle is a show-stopping dessert with the perfect balance of rich chocolate and refreshing orange flavors!

**Chocolate Cherry Smoothie**

*Ingredients:*

- 1 cup frozen dark sweet cherries, pitted
- 1 ripe banana
- 1 cup unsweetened almond milk (or milk of your choice)
- 2 tablespoons unsweetened cocoa powder
- 1 tablespoon almond butter
- 1 teaspoon honey or maple syrup (optional, depending on sweetness preference)
- Ice cubes (optional)

*Instructions:*

Place the frozen cherries, ripe banana, almond milk, unsweetened cocoa powder, and almond butter in a blender.
If you prefer a sweeter smoothie, add honey or maple syrup to taste.
Blend all the ingredients until smooth and creamy.
If you'd like a colder smoothie, you can add ice cubes and blend again until well combined.
Pour the Chocolate Cherry Smoothie into a glass.
Optionally, garnish with a few additional cherries or a sprinkle of cocoa powder.
Serve immediately and enjoy this delicious and nutritious smoothie!

Feel free to customize the recipe by adding a scoop of protein powder or adjusting the sweetness level to suit your taste. Include any tips for achieving the perfect texture and flavor in your cookbook. This Chocolate Cherry Smoothie is a delightful way to enjoy the combination of chocolate and cherries in a healthy and refreshing drink!

**Chocolate Pretzel Bark**

*Ingredients:*

- 12 oz semisweet or dark chocolate, finely chopped
- 2 cups pretzels, broken into pieces
- 1/2 cup unsalted peanuts (optional)
- Sea salt for sprinkling (optional)
- 1/4 cup white chocolate chips (optional, for drizzling)

*Instructions:*

Line a baking sheet with parchment paper or a silicone baking mat.
In a heatproof bowl, melt the semisweet or dark chocolate using a double boiler or by microwaving in short intervals, stirring each time until smooth.
Once the chocolate is fully melted, spread it evenly onto the prepared baking sheet.
Sprinkle the broken pretzel pieces and peanuts (if using) evenly over the melted chocolate, pressing them gently into the chocolate.
If desired, sprinkle a pinch of sea salt over the top for a sweet and salty flavor.
In a microwave-safe bowl, melt the white chocolate chips in short intervals, stirring each time until smooth.
Drizzle the melted white chocolate over the chocolate and pretzel layer.
Place the baking sheet in the refrigerator for about 1 hour or until the chocolate is completely set.
Once set, break the Chocolate Pretzel Bark into smaller pieces.
Store in an airtight container in a cool place or the refrigerator.
Enjoy this delightful and addictive Chocolate Pretzel Bark as a snack or a homemade gift!

Feel free to experiment by adding dried fruits, different types of nuts, or even a sprinkle of festive decorations for special occasions. Include any tips for achieving the perfect balance of sweetness and crunch in your cookbook. This Chocolate Pretzel Bark is a simple yet irresistible treat!

**Chocolate Mint Brownies**

*Ingredients:*

For the Brownie Layer:

- 1 cup unsalted butter, melted
- 2 cups granulated sugar
- 4 large eggs
- 1 teaspoon vanilla extract
- 1/2 cup unsweetened cocoa powder
- 1 cup all-purpose flour
- 1/2 teaspoon baking powder
- 1/4 teaspoon salt

For the Mint Layer:

- 3 cups powdered sugar
- 1/2 cup unsalted butter, softened
- 2 tablespoons milk
- 1/2 teaspoon peppermint extract
- Green food coloring (optional)

For the Chocolate Ganache Topping:

- 6 oz semisweet chocolate, finely chopped
- 1/2 cup heavy cream
- 1 tablespoon unsalted butter

*Instructions:*

For the Brownie Layer:

>Preheat your oven to 350°F (175°C). Grease a 9x13-inch baking pan or line it with parchment paper.
>In a large bowl, combine the melted butter and granulated sugar. Stir until well combined.
>Add the eggs and vanilla extract to the butter-sugar mixture. Mix until smooth.
>In a separate bowl, whisk together the cocoa powder, flour, baking powder, and salt.

Gradually add the dry ingredients to the wet ingredients, mixing until just combined.
Spread the brownie batter evenly in the prepared baking pan.
Bake in the preheated oven for 25-30 minutes or until a toothpick inserted into the center comes out with moist crumbs (not wet batter). Allow the brownies to cool completely.

For the Mint Layer:

In a medium bowl, beat together the powdered sugar, softened butter, milk, peppermint extract, and green food coloring (if using) until smooth and creamy.
Spread the mint layer evenly over the cooled brownies.

For the Chocolate Ganache Topping:

In a heatproof bowl, combine the finely chopped semisweet chocolate, heavy cream, and butter.
Heat the mixture in the microwave or using a double boiler, stirring until the chocolate is completely melted and the ganache is smooth.
Pour the chocolate ganache over the mint layer, spreading it evenly with a spatula.
Allow the ganache to set at room temperature or place the brownies in the refrigerator for faster setting.
Once set, cut the Chocolate Mint Brownies into squares.
Serve and enjoy these decadent and minty brownies!

Feel free to add a sprinkle of crushed peppermint candies on top for extra decoration. Include any tips for achieving the perfect layers and flavors in your cookbook. These Chocolate Mint Brownies are a delightful combination of rich chocolate and refreshing mint!

**Chocolate Caramel Popcorn**

*Ingredients:*

- 12 cups popped popcorn (about 1/2 cup unpopped kernels)
- 1 cup unsalted butter
- 1 cup packed brown sugar
- 1/2 cup light corn syrup
- 1/2 teaspoon salt
- 1/4 teaspoon baking soda
- 1/2 teaspoon vanilla extract
- 1 cup semisweet or dark chocolate chips
- 1/2 cup chopped nuts (optional)

*Instructions:*

Preheat your oven to 250°F (120°C). Line two large baking sheets with parchment paper or silicone baking mats.

Place the popped popcorn in a large mixing bowl, removing any unpopped kernels.

In a saucepan over medium heat, melt the butter. Stir in the brown sugar, corn syrup, and salt.

Bring the mixture to a boil, stirring constantly. Once it reaches a boil, let it cook without stirring for 4-5 minutes.

Remove the saucepan from heat and stir in the baking soda and vanilla extract. The mixture will bubble up, so be cautious.

Pour the caramel sauce over the popcorn, using a spatula to gently toss and coat the popcorn evenly.

Divide the coated popcorn between the prepared baking sheets, spreading it out into an even layer.

Bake in the preheated oven for 45-60 minutes, stirring every 15 minutes to ensure even coating.

While the popcorn is baking, melt the chocolate chips in a heatproof bowl, either using a microwave or a double boiler.

Once the popcorn is done baking, remove it from the oven and drizzle the melted chocolate over the top. Add chopped nuts if desired.

Allow the Chocolate Caramel Popcorn to cool completely before breaking it into clusters.

Store in an airtight container.

Serve and enjoy this sweet and crunchy Chocolate Caramel Popcorn as a delightful treat!

Feel free to customize the recipe by adding your favorite nuts, pretzels, or even dried fruit. Include any tips for achieving the perfect balance of sweetness and crunch in your cookbook. This Chocolate Caramel Popcorn is a perfect combination of caramel goodness and chocolatey decadence!

**Chocolate Pistachio Torte**

*Ingredients:*

For the Torte:

- 1 cup shelled pistachios, finely ground
- 1 cup granulated sugar
- 1/2 cup all-purpose flour
- 1/4 cup unsweetened cocoa powder
- 1 teaspoon baking powder
- 1/2 teaspoon salt
- 1/2 cup unsalted butter, melted and cooled
- 4 large eggs
- 1 teaspoon vanilla extract

For the Chocolate Ganache:

- 6 oz dark chocolate, finely chopped
- 1/2 cup heavy cream
- 1 tablespoon unsalted butter

For Garnish:

- Chopped pistachios
- Powdered sugar

*Instructions:*

For the Torte:

> Preheat your oven to 350°F (175°C). Grease a 9-inch springform pan and line the bottom with parchment paper.
> In a food processor, grind the shelled pistachios until fine.
> In a bowl, whisk together the ground pistachios, sugar, flour, cocoa powder, baking powder, and salt.

In another bowl, whisk together the melted butter, eggs, and vanilla extract.
Add the wet ingredients to the dry ingredients and mix until well combined.
Pour the batter into the prepared springform pan and spread it evenly.
Bake in the preheated oven for about 25-30 minutes or until a toothpick inserted into the center comes out with moist crumbs.
Allow the torte to cool in the pan for 10 minutes, then transfer it to a wire rack to cool completely.

For the Chocolate Ganache:

Place the finely chopped dark chocolate in a heatproof bowl.
In a saucepan, heat the heavy cream until it just begins to simmer.
Pour the hot cream over the chocolate. Let it sit for a minute, then stir until the chocolate is completely melted and the mixture is smooth.
Stir in the butter until well combined.
Allow the ganache to cool slightly before pouring it over the cooled pistachio torte.
Spread the ganache evenly over the top of the torte.

For Garnish:

Sprinkle chopped pistachios over the ganache.
Optionally, dust the top with powdered sugar for a decorative touch.
Allow the ganache to set before slicing and serving.
Enjoy this decadent Chocolate Pistachio Torte!

Include any tips for achieving the perfect texture and flavor in your cookbook. This Chocolate Pistachio Torte is a delightful combination of rich chocolate and the nutty flavor of pistachios!

**Chocolate Hazelnut Spread**

*Ingredients:*

- 2 cups roasted hazelnuts
- 1 cup powdered sugar
- 1/3 cup unsweetened cocoa powder
- 1/4 teaspoon salt
- 1 teaspoon vanilla extract
- 1/4 cup vegetable oil or hazelnut oil
- 1/2 cup semisweet chocolate chips, melted (optional, for added richness)

*Instructions:*

Start by roasting the hazelnuts. Preheat your oven to 350°F (175°C). Spread the hazelnuts on a baking sheet and roast for about 10-12 minutes, or until the skins start to crack. Allow them to cool slightly.

Once the hazelnuts are slightly cooled, rub them between your hands or in a clean kitchen towel to remove the skins. Some skin remaining is okay.

In a food processor, blend the roasted hazelnuts until they form a smooth hazelnut butter. This may take several minutes, and you may need to scrape down the sides of the food processor.

Add the powdered sugar, cocoa powder, salt, and vanilla extract to the hazelnut butter. Blend until well combined.

With the food processor running, slowly stream in the vegetable oil or hazelnut oil until the mixture reaches a smooth and spreadable consistency.

If you want a richer flavor, melt the semisweet chocolate chips and add them to the mixture. Blend until smooth.

Taste the chocolate hazelnut spread and adjust the sweetness or thickness according to your preference by adding more sugar or oil.

Transfer the chocolate hazelnut spread to a jar or airtight container.

Store in a cool, dark place or in the refrigerator. The spread will thicken slightly when chilled.

Enjoy your homemade Chocolate Hazelnut Spread on toast, pancakes, waffles, or as a dip for fruit!

Feel free to customize the recipe by adjusting the sweetness or adding more cocoa powder for a richer chocolate flavor. Include any tips for achieving the perfect consistency and flavor in your cookbook. This Chocolate Hazelnut Spread is a delightful and versatile treat!

**Chocolate Raspberry Cupcakes**

*Ingredients:*

For the Cupcakes:

- 1 cup all-purpose flour
- 1/2 cup unsweetened cocoa powder
- 1 teaspoon baking powder
- 1/2 teaspoon baking soda
- 1/4 teaspoon salt
- 1/2 cup unsalted butter, softened
- 3/4 cup granulated sugar
- 2 large eggs
- 1 teaspoon vanilla extract
- 1/2 cup buttermilk
- 1/2 cup raspberry puree (made by blending fresh or thawed frozen raspberries)

For the Raspberry Buttercream Frosting:

- 1 cup unsalted butter, softened
- 3 cups powdered sugar
- 1/2 cup raspberry puree
- 1 teaspoon vanilla extract
- Fresh raspberries for garnish (optional)

*Instructions:*

For the Cupcakes:

> Preheat your oven to 350°F (175°C). Line a cupcake tin with paper liners.
> In a bowl, whisk together the flour, cocoa powder, baking powder, baking soda, and salt.
> In a separate large bowl, cream together the softened butter and granulated sugar until light and fluffy.
> Add the eggs one at a time, beating well after each addition. Stir in the vanilla extract.
> Gradually add the dry ingredients to the wet ingredients, alternating with buttermilk, beginning and ending with the dry ingredients. Mix until just combined.

Gently fold in the raspberry puree until evenly distributed.
Divide the batter evenly among the cupcake liners, filling each about 2/3 full.
Bake in the preheated oven for 18-20 minutes, or until a toothpick inserted into the center comes out clean.
Allow the cupcakes to cool in the tin for 5 minutes, then transfer them to a wire rack to cool completely.

For the Raspberry Buttercream Frosting:

In a large bowl, beat the softened butter until creamy.
Gradually add the powdered sugar, one cup at a time, beating well after each addition.
Add the raspberry puree and vanilla extract. Beat until smooth and fluffy.
If needed, adjust the consistency by adding more powdered sugar or a splash of milk.

Assembly:

Once the cupcakes are completely cooled, pipe or spread the raspberry buttercream frosting on top of each cupcake.
Optionally, garnish with fresh raspberries.
Serve and enjoy these delightful Chocolate Raspberry Cupcakes!

Feel free to get creative with the decoration or add a chocolate drizzle for an extra touch. Include any tips for achieving moist cupcakes and vibrant raspberry flavor in your cookbook. These cupcakes are a perfect combination of rich chocolate and fruity raspberry goodness!

**Rocky Road Chocolate Bars**

*Ingredients:*

- 1 cup unsalted butter
- 2 cups semisweet chocolate chips
- 1 cup granulated sugar
- 3 large eggs
- 1 teaspoon vanilla extract
- 1 1/2 cups all-purpose flour
- 1/4 cup unsweetened cocoa powder
- 1/2 teaspoon baking powder
- 1/4 teaspoon salt
- 1 cup chopped walnuts or pecans
- 1 1/2 cups mini marshmallows
- 1 cup chocolate chunks or additional chocolate chips

*Instructions:*

Preheat your oven to 350°F (175°C). Grease and line a 9x13-inch baking pan with parchment paper.
In a saucepan over low heat, melt the butter and semisweet chocolate chips, stirring until smooth. Remove from heat and let it cool slightly.
In a large bowl, whisk together the granulated sugar, eggs, and vanilla extract until well combined.
Add the melted chocolate mixture to the sugar and egg mixture, stirring until smooth.
In a separate bowl, sift together the flour, cocoa powder, baking powder, and salt.
Gradually add the dry ingredients to the wet ingredients, mixing until just combined.
Fold in the chopped nuts, mini marshmallows, and chocolate chunks.
Spread the batter evenly into the prepared baking pan.
Bake in the preheated oven for 25-30 minutes or until a toothpick inserted into the center comes out with moist crumbs.
Remove the pan from the oven and let it cool completely in the pan on a wire rack.
Once cooled, lift the Rocky Road Chocolate Bars out of the pan using the parchment paper and place them on a cutting board.
Cut into squares or bars using a sharp knife.

Serve and enjoy these decadent Rocky Road Chocolate Bars!

Feel free to customize the recipe by adding other mix-ins like shredded coconut or different types of nuts. Include any tips for achieving the perfect balance of chewiness and crunch in your cookbook. These Rocky Road Chocolate Bars are a delightful combination of rich chocolate, nuts, and gooey marshmallows!

**Chocolate Almond Joy Bites**

*Ingredients:*

- 1 cup shredded coconut (sweetened or unsweetened)
- 1/2 cup almond flour
- 1/4 cup maple syrup or honey
- 1/4 cup coconut oil, melted
- 1 teaspoon vanilla extract
- 1/4 teaspoon almond extract
- Pinch of salt
- 1 cup semisweet or dark chocolate chips
- 1/4 cup whole almonds

*Instructions:*

In a mixing bowl, combine the shredded coconut, almond flour, maple syrup or honey, melted coconut oil, vanilla extract, almond extract, and a pinch of salt. Mix until well combined.

Place the mixture in the refrigerator for about 15-20 minutes to firm up.

After the mixture has chilled, use your hands to form small bite-sized balls or shapes. Press a whole almond into the center of each bite.

Place the shaped bites on a parchment paper-lined tray and return them to the refrigerator.

In a heatproof bowl, melt the chocolate chips using a double boiler or by microwaving in short intervals, stirring each time until smooth.

Using a fork or toothpick, dip each coconut-almond bite into the melted chocolate, ensuring it's fully coated. Allow any excess chocolate to drip off.

Place the coated bites back on the parchment paper-lined tray.

Once all the bites are coated, place the tray in the refrigerator for about 30 minutes or until the chocolate is set.

Once set, transfer the Chocolate Almond Joy Bites to an airtight container.

Store in the refrigerator until ready to serve.

Enjoy these delightful and indulgent Chocolate Almond Joy Bites!

Feel free to customize the recipe by adding a sprinkle of shredded coconut or chopped almonds on top of the chocolate coating. Include any tips for achieving the perfect texture and flavor in your cookbook. These Chocolate Almond Joy Bites are a bite-sized treat reminiscent of the classic candy bar!

**Chocolate Cinnamon Rolls**

*Ingredients:*

For the Dough:

- 1 cup warm milk (110°F/43°C)
- 2 1/4 teaspoons active dry yeast
- 1/4 cup granulated sugar
- 1/4 cup unsalted butter, melted
- 1 teaspoon vanilla extract
- 1 large egg
- 4 cups all-purpose flour
- 1/2 teaspoon salt

For the Chocolate Filling:

- 1/2 cup unsalted butter, softened
- 1 cup brown sugar, packed
- 2 tablespoons unsweetened cocoa powder
- 1 tablespoon ground cinnamon
- 1/2 cup semisweet chocolate chips or chunks

For the Chocolate Glaze:

- 1 cup powdered sugar
- 2 tablespoons unsweetened cocoa powder
- 2-3 tablespoons milk
- 1/2 teaspoon vanilla extract

*Instructions:*

For the Dough:

In a small bowl, combine warm milk and active dry yeast. Let it sit for about 5 minutes, or until foamy.
In a large mixing bowl, combine the yeast mixture, granulated sugar, melted butter, vanilla extract, and egg.
Add in the flour and salt. Mix until a dough forms.
Knead the dough on a floured surface until it becomes smooth and elastic.

Place the dough in a greased bowl, cover it with a clean kitchen towel, and let it rise in a warm place for about 1-2 hours, or until it has doubled in size.

For the Chocolate Filling:

In a bowl, mix together the softened butter, brown sugar, cocoa powder, and ground cinnamon until well combined.
Roll out the risen dough on a floured surface into a rectangle.
Spread the chocolate filling evenly over the dough, leaving a small border around the edges.
Sprinkle the semisweet chocolate chips or chunks over the filling.
Starting from one long edge, roll the dough into a log.
Cut the log into equal-sized rolls.
Place the rolls in a greased baking dish, leaving some space between each.
Cover the dish with a kitchen towel and let the rolls rise for about 30-45 minutes.

Baking:

Preheat your oven to 350°F (175°C).
Bake the Chocolate Cinnamon Rolls in the preheated oven for 20-25 minutes, or until they are golden brown.
Remove from the oven and let them cool slightly.

For the Chocolate Glaze:

In a bowl, whisk together the powdered sugar, cocoa powder, milk, and vanilla extract until smooth.
Drizzle the chocolate glaze over the warm rolls.
Serve and enjoy these delicious Chocolate Cinnamon Rolls!

Feel free to customize the recipe by adding chopped nuts or more chocolate to the filling. Include any tips for achieving soft and gooey cinnamon rolls in your cookbook. These Chocolate Cinnamon Rolls are a decadent twist on the classic!

**Chocolate Covered Cherry Cheesecake**

*Ingredients:*

For the Chocolate Crust:

- 1 1/2 cups chocolate cookie crumbs (from about 20 chocolate sandwich cookies)
- 1/3 cup unsalted butter, melted

For the Cherry Cheesecake Filling:

- 3 cups fresh or frozen cherries, pitted and halved
- 1/2 cup granulated sugar
- 2 tablespoons cornstarch
- 1 tablespoon lemon juice
- 4 packages (8 oz each) cream cheese, softened
- 1 cup granulated sugar
- 4 large eggs
- 1 teaspoon vanilla extract
- 1/2 cup sour cream
- 1/2 cup cherry juice (reserved from the prepared cherries)

For the Chocolate Ganache Topping:

- 6 oz semisweet or dark chocolate, finely chopped
- 1/2 cup heavy cream
- 1 tablespoon unsalted butter

*Instructions:*

For the Chocolate Crust:

Preheat your oven to 325°F (163°C). Grease a 9-inch springform pan.
In a bowl, mix the chocolate cookie crumbs and melted butter until the crumbs are evenly coated.

Press the mixture into the bottom of the springform pan to form the crust.
Bake the crust in the preheated oven for 10 minutes. Allow it to cool while you prepare the filling.

For the Cherry Cheesecake Filling:

In a saucepan, combine the pitted and halved cherries, granulated sugar, cornstarch, and lemon juice. Cook over medium heat, stirring occasionally, until the mixture thickens and the cherries release their juices. Remove from heat and let it cool.
Once cooled, strain the cherry mixture, reserving the juice for later use.
In a large mixing bowl, beat the softened cream cheese until smooth.
Add the granulated sugar and continue to beat until well combined.
Add the eggs one at a time, beating well after each addition.
Mix in the vanilla extract, sour cream, and 1/2 cup of the reserved cherry juice.
Pour half of the cream cheese mixture over the chocolate crust.
Spoon half of the prepared cherry mixture over the cream cheese layer.
Repeat with the remaining cream cheese and cherry layers.
Use a knife or skewer to gently swirl the layers for a marbled effect.
Bake the cheesecake in the preheated oven for 50-60 minutes, or until the center is set and the top is lightly browned.
Allow the cheesecake to cool in the pan, then refrigerate for at least 4 hours or overnight.

For the Chocolate Ganache Topping:

In a heatproof bowl, combine the finely chopped semisweet or dark chocolate, heavy cream, and butter.
Heat the mixture in the microwave or using a double boiler, stirring until the chocolate is completely melted and the ganache is smooth.
Pour the chocolate ganache over the chilled cheesecake, spreading it evenly.
Allow the ganache to set before slicing and serving.
Serve and enjoy this decadent Chocolate Covered Cherry Cheesecake!

Feel free to garnish the cheesecake with additional fresh cherries or chocolate shavings. Include any tips for achieving the perfect texture and flavor in your cookbook.

This Chocolate Covered Cherry Cheesecake is a luscious and indulgent dessert!

**Chocolate Strawberry Shortcake**

*Ingredients:*

For the Chocolate Shortcakes:

- 2 cups all-purpose flour
- 1/2 cup unsweetened cocoa powder
- 1/3 cup granulated sugar
- 1 tablespoon baking powder
- 1/2 teaspoon salt
- 1/2 cup unsalted butter, cold and cut into small cubes
- 1 cup milk
- 1 teaspoon vanilla extract

For the Chocolate Whipped Cream:

- 2 cups heavy cream
- 1/2 cup powdered sugar
- 2 tablespoons unsweetened cocoa powder
- 1 teaspoon vanilla extract

For the Strawberry Topping:

- 3 cups fresh strawberries, hulled and sliced
- 1/4 cup granulated sugar
- 1 teaspoon lemon juice

*Instructions:*

For the Chocolate Shortcakes:

Preheat your oven to 425°F (220°C). Line a baking sheet with parchment paper. In a large bowl, whisk together the flour, cocoa powder, granulated sugar, baking powder, and salt.

Add the cold, cubed butter to the dry ingredients. Use a pastry cutter or your fingertips to cut the butter into the flour mixture until it resembles coarse crumbs.
In a separate bowl, combine the milk and vanilla extract.
Pour the wet ingredients into the dry ingredients and stir until just combined.
Turn the dough out onto a floured surface and gently knead it a few times until it comes together.
Pat the dough into a 3/4-inch thick rectangle and use a round biscuit cutter to cut out shortcakes.
Place the shortcakes on the prepared baking sheet and bake for 12-15 minutes, or until they are firm to the touch.
Allow the shortcakes to cool on a wire rack.

For the Chocolate Whipped Cream:

In a chilled bowl, whip the heavy cream until soft peaks form.
Sift in the powdered sugar and cocoa powder. Add the vanilla extract.
Continue to whip until stiff peaks form. Be careful not to overmix.

For the Strawberry Topping:

In a bowl, combine the sliced strawberries, granulated sugar, and lemon juice.
Toss until the strawberries are coated in sugar.
Let the strawberry mixture sit for about 15 minutes to allow the flavors to meld.

Assembly:

Slice the chocolate shortcakes in half horizontally.
Spoon some of the strawberry mixture onto the bottom half of each shortcake.
Dollop a generous amount of chocolate whipped cream over the strawberries.
Place the top half of the shortcake over the whipped cream.
Garnish with additional strawberries or a dusting of cocoa powder.
Serve and enjoy this delightful Chocolate Strawberry Shortcake!

Include any tips for achieving light and fluffy shortcakes and perfect whipped cream in your cookbook. This Chocolate Strawberry Shortcake is a delightful twist on the classic dessert!

**Chocolate Bread Pudding**

*Ingredients:*

- 6 cups cubed day-old bread (such as French or brioche)
- 1 1/2 cups semisweet or dark chocolate chips
- 4 cups whole milk
- 4 large eggs
- 1 cup granulated sugar
- 1/4 cup unsweetened cocoa powder
- 1 teaspoon vanilla extract
- 1/2 teaspoon cinnamon
- 1/4 teaspoon salt
- 1/2 cup chopped nuts (optional, such as pecans or walnuts)

*For the Chocolate Sauce:*

- 1/2 cup heavy cream
- 1 cup semisweet or dark chocolate chips
- 2 tablespoons unsalted butter

*Instructions:*

Preheat your oven to 350°F (175°C). Grease a 9x13-inch baking dish.
In a large bowl, combine the cubed bread and chocolate chips. Spread the mixture evenly in the prepared baking dish.
In a saucepan over medium heat, warm the milk until it's just about to simmer. Remove from heat.
In a separate bowl, whisk together the eggs, granulated sugar, cocoa powder, vanilla extract, cinnamon, and salt.
Slowly pour the warm milk into the egg mixture, whisking constantly to avoid curdling the eggs.
Pour the egg and milk mixture over the bread and chocolate chips in the baking dish. Gently press down on the bread to ensure it absorbs the liquid.
Let the mixture sit for about 15-20 minutes to allow the bread to soak up the custard.
If desired, sprinkle chopped nuts over the top of the bread pudding.
Bake in the preheated oven for 45-50 minutes, or until the center is set and the top is golden brown.

*For the Chocolate Sauce:*

In a small saucepan, heat the heavy cream until it just begins to simmer.
Remove from heat and add the chocolate chips and butter. Stir until melted and smooth.
Pour the warm chocolate sauce over individual servings of the bread pudding.
Serve and enjoy this decadent Chocolate Bread Pudding!

Feel free to serve the bread pudding warm or at room temperature. Include any tips for achieving the perfect balance of chocolatey richness and creamy custard in your cookbook. This Chocolate Bread Pudding is a comforting and indulgent dessert!

**Chocolate Peppermint Bark**

Ingredients:

12 oz semisweet or dark chocolate, chopped

12 oz white chocolate, chopped

1/2 teaspoon peppermint extract

Crushed peppermint candies or candy canes

Instructions:

Line a baking sheet with parchment paper.

In a heatproof bowl, melt the semisweet or dark chocolate either using a double boiler or in the microwave in short intervals, stirring each time until smooth.

Once melted, stir in the peppermint extract until well combined.

Pour the melted semisweet or dark chocolate onto the prepared baking sheet and spread it into an even layer using a spatula.

Place the baking sheet in the refrigerator to allow the chocolate to set while you prepare the white chocolate layer.

In another heatproof bowl, melt the white chocolate using the same method as before.

Once melted, stir in the peppermint extract until well combined.

Pour the melted white chocolate over the set semisweet or dark chocolate layer and spread it evenly.

Immediately sprinkle crushed peppermint candies or candy cane pieces over the white chocolate layer before it sets.

Place the baking sheet back in the refrigerator and let the entire bark set completely.

Once set, break the Chocolate Peppermint Bark into irregular pieces.

Serve and enjoy this festive and delicious treat!

Feel free to get creative by adding swirls or layers to the bark, or even incorporating different types of chocolate. Include any tips for achieving a smooth and glossy finish in your cookbook. This Chocolate Peppermint Bark is a perfect holiday treat with a delightful combination of chocolate and peppermint flavors!

**Chocolate Toffee Crunch Cookies**

*Ingredients:*

- 1 cup unsalted butter, softened
- 1 cup granulated sugar
- 1 cup brown sugar, packed
- 2 large eggs
- 1 teaspoon vanilla extract
- 2 cups all-purpose flour
- 1/2 cup unsweetened cocoa powder
- 1 teaspoon baking soda
- 1/2 teaspoon salt
- 1 cup semisweet chocolate chips
- 1 cup toffee bits
- 1/2 cup chopped nuts (optional)

*Instructions:*

Preheat your oven to 350°F (175°C). Line baking sheets with parchment paper.
In a large bowl, cream together the softened butter, granulated sugar, and brown sugar until light and fluffy.
Add the eggs one at a time, beating well after each addition.
Stir in the vanilla extract.
In a separate bowl, whisk together the flour, cocoa powder, baking soda, and salt.
Gradually add the dry ingredients to the wet ingredients, mixing until just combined.
Fold in the semisweet chocolate chips, toffee bits, and chopped nuts (if using).
Drop rounded tablespoons of dough onto the prepared baking sheets, spacing them about 2 inches apart.
Bake in the preheated oven for 10-12 minutes, or until the edges are set but the centers are still soft.
Allow the cookies to cool on the baking sheets for a few minutes before transferring them to a wire rack to cool completely.
Once cooled, store the Chocolate Toffee Crunch Cookies in an airtight container.
Serve and enjoy these delightful cookies with a perfect combination of chocolate and toffee crunch!

Feel free to customize the recipe by adding different types of nuts or adjusting the ratio of chocolate chips to toffee bits. Include any tips for achieving a chewy or crispy texture in your cookbook. These Chocolate Toffee Crunch Cookies are a sweet and satisfying treat!

Chocolate Pumpkin Pie

*Ingredients:*

For the Chocolate Pie Crust:

- 1 1/4 cups all-purpose flour
- 1/4 cup unsweetened cocoa powder
- 1/2 cup unsalted butter, cold and cut into small cubes
- 1/4 cup granulated sugar
- 1/4 teaspoon salt
- 2-3 tablespoons cold water

For the Pumpkin Filling:

- 1 can (15 oz) pumpkin puree
- 2/3 cup brown sugar, packed
- 1 teaspoon ground cinnamon
- 1/2 teaspoon ground ginger
- 1/4 teaspoon ground nutmeg
- 1/4 teaspoon ground cloves
- 1/2 teaspoon salt
- 3 large eggs
- 1 cup heavy cream
- 1 teaspoon vanilla extract

For the Chocolate Ganache Topping:

- 4 oz semisweet or dark chocolate, finely chopped
- 1/2 cup heavy cream
- 1 tablespoon unsalted butter

*Instructions:*

For the Chocolate Pie Crust:

In a food processor, combine the flour, cocoa powder, granulated sugar, and salt. Pulse a few times to mix.

Add the cold, cubed butter to the processor and pulse until the mixture resembles coarse crumbs.

Gradually add cold water, one tablespoon at a time, pulsing until the dough starts to come together.

Turn the dough out onto a lightly floured surface and knead it a few times until it forms a ball.

Flatten the ball into a disc, wrap it in plastic wrap, and refrigerate for at least 30 minutes.

Preheat your oven to 375°F (190°C).

Roll out the chilled dough on a floured surface to fit a 9-inch pie pan.

Transfer the rolled-out dough to the pie pan, trim the excess, and crimp the edges.

For the Pumpkin Filling:

In a large bowl, whisk together the pumpkin puree, brown sugar, cinnamon, ginger, nutmeg, cloves, and salt.

Add the eggs one at a time, whisking well after each addition.

Stir in the heavy cream and vanilla extract until the filling is smooth.

Pour the pumpkin filling into the prepared chocolate pie crust.

Bake in the preheated oven for 45-50 minutes or until the center is set.

Allow the pie to cool completely on a wire rack.

For the Chocolate Ganache Topping:

In a heatproof bowl, combine the finely chopped semisweet or dark chocolate, heavy cream, and butter.

Heat the mixture in the microwave or using a double boiler, stirring until the chocolate is completely melted and the ganache is smooth.

Pour the warm chocolate ganache over the cooled pumpkin pie, spreading it evenly.

Allow the ganache to set before slicing and serving.

Serve and enjoy this decadent Chocolate Pumpkin Pie!

Feel free to garnish the pie with whipped cream or chocolate shavings for an extra touch. Include any tips for achieving a flaky crust and perfectly spiced pumpkin filling in your cookbook. This Chocolate Pumpkin Pie is a delightful twist on a classic fall dessert!

**Chocolate Marshmallow Fudge**

*Ingredients:*

- 3 cups semisweet chocolate chips
- 1 can (14 oz) sweetened condensed milk
- 1/4 cup unsalted butter
- 1 teaspoon vanilla extract
- 2 cups miniature marshmallows
- 1 cup chopped nuts (optional, such as walnuts or pecans)

*Instructions:*

Line an 8-inch square baking pan with parchment paper, leaving some overhang on the sides for easy removal.
In a saucepan over low heat, combine the chocolate chips, sweetened condensed milk, and butter. Stir continuously until the chocolate chips and butter are completely melted and the mixture is smooth.
Remove the saucepan from heat and stir in the vanilla extract.
Allow the chocolate mixture to cool slightly, then fold in the miniature marshmallows and chopped nuts (if using). The marshmallows will partially melt, creating a delightful texture.
Pour the fudge mixture into the prepared baking pan, spreading it evenly.
Refrigerate the fudge for at least 2-3 hours or until it is set.
Once set, use the parchment paper overhang to lift the fudge out of the pan.
Place the fudge on a cutting board and cut it into squares or desired shapes.
Store the Chocolate Marshmallow Fudge in an airtight container in the refrigerator.
Serve and enjoy this sweet and gooey treat!

Feel free to customize the recipe by adding other mix-ins like crushed cookies or drizzling melted white chocolate on top. Include any tips for achieving the perfect balance of chocolate and marshmallow in your cookbook. This Chocolate Marshmallow Fudge is a simple and delightful dessert that's sure to satisfy your sweet tooth!

**Chocolate Raspberry Scones**

*Ingredients:*

- 2 cups all-purpose flour
- 1/4 cup granulated sugar
- 1 tablespoon baking powder
- 1/2 teaspoon salt
- 1/2 cup unsalted butter, cold and cut into small pieces
- 1/2 cup semisweet chocolate chips or chunks
- 1/2 cup fresh raspberries
- 2/3 cup milk (plus extra for brushing)
- 1 teaspoon vanilla extract
- Zest of 1 lemon
- Powdered sugar for dusting (optional)

*Instructions:*

Preheat your oven to 425°F (220°C). Line a baking sheet with parchment paper.
In a large bowl, whisk together the flour, granulated sugar, baking powder, and salt.
Add the cold, cubed butter to the dry ingredients. Use a pastry cutter or your fingertips to cut the butter into the flour mixture until it resembles coarse crumbs.
Stir in the semisweet chocolate chips or chunks and fresh raspberries.
In a separate bowl, mix together the milk, vanilla extract, and lemon zest.
Gradually add the wet ingredients to the dry ingredients, stirring until just combined.
Turn the dough out onto a floured surface and knead it gently a few times until it comes together.
Pat the dough into a circle about 1 inch thick.
Use a round biscuit cutter to cut out scones from the dough. Place the scones on the prepared baking sheet.
Brush the tops of the scones with a little milk.
Bake in the preheated oven for 12-15 minutes or until the scones are golden brown.
Allow the scones to cool on a wire rack.
If desired, dust the cooled scones with powdered sugar before serving.
Serve and enjoy these delightful Chocolate Raspberry Scones!

Feel free to customize the recipe by adding a drizzle of chocolate glaze or a sprinkle of additional raspberries on top. Include any tips for achieving light and flaky scones in your cookbook. These Chocolate Raspberry Scones are a perfect combination of rich chocolate and tart raspberries!

**Chocolate Pecan Pie Bars**

*Ingredients:*

For the Crust:

- 1 1/2 cups all-purpose flour
- 1/2 cup unsalted butter, cold and cut into small pieces
- 1/4 cup granulated sugar
- 1/4 teaspoon salt

For the Pecan Filling:

- 1/2 cup unsalted butter
- 1 cup packed brown sugar
- 1/3 cup honey or maple syrup
- 2 tablespoons heavy cream
- 2 cups chopped pecans
- 1 teaspoon vanilla extract

For the Chocolate Layer:

- 1 cup semisweet chocolate chips
- 2 tablespoons unsalted butter

*Instructions:*

For the Crust:

> Preheat your oven to 350°F (175°C). Line a 9x9-inch baking pan with parchment paper, leaving some overhang on the sides for easy removal.
> In a food processor, combine the flour, cold butter, granulated sugar, and salt. Pulse until the mixture resembles coarse crumbs.
> Press the mixture into the bottom of the prepared baking pan to form the crust. Bake in the preheated oven for 15-18 minutes or until the edges are lightly golden.

Allow the crust to cool while you prepare the pecan filling.

For the Pecan Filling:

In a saucepan over medium heat, melt the butter.
Stir in the brown sugar, honey or maple syrup, and heavy cream. Bring the mixture to a boil, stirring constantly.
Remove the saucepan from heat and stir in the chopped pecans and vanilla extract.
Pour the pecan filling over the cooled crust, spreading it evenly.

For the Chocolate Layer:

In a microwave-safe bowl, melt the chocolate chips and butter in short intervals, stirring each time until smooth.
Drizzle the melted chocolate over the pecan filling in the pan.
Use a knife or skewer to create swirls or patterns with the chocolate.
Place the baking pan in the refrigerator for at least 2 hours or until the bars are set.
Once set, use the parchment paper overhang to lift the bars out of the pan.
Place them on a cutting board and cut into squares.
Serve and enjoy these decadent Chocolate Pecan Pie Bars!

Feel free to customize the recipe by adding a sprinkle of sea salt over the chocolate layer or incorporating different types of nuts. Include any tips for achieving the perfect balance of sweetness and crunch in your cookbook. These Chocolate Pecan Pie Bars are a delightful twist on a classic dessert!

**Chocolate Espresso Brownies**

*Ingredients:*

- 1 cup unsalted butter
- 1 and 1/2 cups granulated sugar
- 4 large eggs
- 1 teaspoon vanilla extract
- 1/2 cup all-purpose flour
- 1/2 cup unsweetened cocoa powder
- 1/4 teaspoon salt
- 2 tablespoons finely ground espresso or coffee powder
- 1 cup semisweet chocolate chips or chunks

*Instructions:*

Preheat your oven to 350°F (175°C). Grease and flour a 9x9-inch baking pan or line it with parchment paper.
In a saucepan over low heat, melt the butter.
Remove the melted butter from heat and stir in the granulated sugar until well combined.
In a large mixing bowl, whisk the eggs and vanilla extract.
Slowly pour the melted butter and sugar mixture into the eggs, stirring continuously to avoid curdling.
In a separate bowl, sift together the flour, cocoa powder, and salt.
Gradually add the dry ingredients to the wet ingredients, mixing until just combined.
Stir in the finely ground espresso or coffee powder until evenly distributed in the batter.
Fold in the semisweet chocolate chips or chunks.
Pour the batter into the prepared baking pan, spreading it evenly.
Bake in the preheated oven for 25-30 minutes, or until a toothpick inserted into the center comes out with a few moist crumbs.
Allow the brownies to cool completely in the pan on a wire rack.
Once cooled, cut the brownies into squares or desired shapes.
Serve and enjoy these rich and fudgy Chocolate Espresso Brownies!

Feel free to customize the recipe by adding chopped nuts or a drizzle of chocolate ganache on top. Include any tips for achieving a perfect balance of chocolate and espresso flavors in your cookbook. These Chocolate Espresso Brownies are a delightful treat for coffee and chocolate lovers!

**Chocolate Caramel Brownie Trifle**

*Ingredients:*

For the Brownies:

- 1 cup unsalted butter
- 2 cups granulated sugar
- 4 large eggs
- 1 teaspoon vanilla extract
- 1/2 cup unsweetened cocoa powder
- 1 cup all-purpose flour
- 1/2 teaspoon baking powder
- 1/4 teaspoon salt

For the Caramel Sauce:

- 1 cup granulated sugar
- 6 tablespoons unsalted butter
- 1/2 cup heavy cream
- 1 teaspoon vanilla extract
- 1/4 teaspoon salt

For the Chocolate Ganache:

- 1 cup semisweet chocolate chips
- 1/2 cup heavy cream

For the Trifle Assembly:

- 2 cups whipped cream (homemade or store-bought)
- Chocolate shavings for garnish (optional)

*Instructions:*

For the Brownies:

> Preheat your oven to 350°F (175°C). Grease and flour a 9x13-inch baking pan. In a saucepan over low heat, melt the butter. Remove from heat and stir in the granulated sugar until well combined.

In a large mixing bowl, whisk the eggs and vanilla extract.
Slowly pour the melted butter and sugar mixture into the eggs, stirring continuously.
In a separate bowl, sift together the cocoa powder, flour, baking powder, and salt.
Gradually add the dry ingredients to the wet ingredients, mixing until just combined.
Pour the brownie batter into the prepared baking pan and spread it evenly.
Bake in the preheated oven for 25-30 minutes, or until a toothpick inserted into the center comes out with a few moist crumbs.
Allow the brownies to cool completely in the pan before cutting them into small cubes.

For the Caramel Sauce:

In a saucepan over medium heat, melt the granulated sugar, stirring constantly until it becomes a golden brown liquid.
Add the butter and stir until melted.
Slowly pour in the heavy cream while stirring continuously. Be cautious, as the mixture may bubble.
Remove the saucepan from heat and stir in the vanilla extract and salt.
Allow the caramel sauce to cool slightly.

For the Chocolate Ganache:

In a heatproof bowl, combine the semisweet chocolate chips and heavy cream.
Heat the mixture in the microwave or using a double boiler, stirring until the chocolate is completely melted and the ganache is smooth.

Trifle Assembly:

In a trifle dish or individual serving glasses, layer cubes of brownies, drizzle with caramel sauce, and spoon over a layer of whipped cream.
Repeat the layers until you reach the top of the trifle dish.
Pour the chocolate ganache over the top layer and spread it evenly.
Garnish with chocolate shavings if desired.
Refrigerate the trifle for at least 2 hours to allow the flavors to meld.
Serve and enjoy this indulgent Chocolate Caramel Brownie Trifle!

Feel free to customize the trifle by adding chopped nuts or additional layers of your favorite ingredients. Include any tips for creating visually appealing layers in your cookbook. This Chocolate Caramel Brownie Trifle is a show-stopping dessert for any occasion!

**Chocolate Pistachio Ice Cream**

*Ingredients:*

- 2 cups shelled and unsalted pistachios
- 2 cups whole milk
- 1 cup heavy cream
- 3/4 cup granulated sugar
- 1/4 cup unsweetened cocoa powder
- 4 large egg yolks
- 1 teaspoon vanilla extract
- 4 oz dark chocolate, chopped

*Instructions:*

Preheat your oven to 350°F (175°C).
Spread the pistachios on a baking sheet and roast them in the preheated oven for about 8-10 minutes, or until fragrant. Allow them to cool.
Once cooled, finely chop half of the roasted pistachios for mixing into the ice cream. Set the remaining half aside for garnish.
In a saucepan, combine the milk, heavy cream, and half of the granulated sugar. Heat the mixture over medium heat, stirring occasionally until it begins to simmer. Do not let it boil.
In a separate bowl, whisk together the egg yolks and the remaining sugar until well combined.
Gradually pour the hot milk mixture into the egg mixture, whisking constantly to avoid curdling.
Return the combined mixture to the saucepan and heat over medium heat, stirring constantly until it thickens and coats the back of a spoon. This forms a custard.
Remove the custard from heat and stir in the chopped pistachios and vanilla extract.
Place the dark chocolate in a heatproof bowl and melt it either in the microwave or using a double boiler.
Pour the melted chocolate into the custard mixture, stirring until well combined.
Allow the mixture to cool to room temperature, then cover and refrigerate it for at least 4 hours or overnight.
Once the custard is chilled, churn it in an ice cream maker according to the manufacturer's instructions.

In the last few minutes of churning, add the reserved roasted pistachios.

Transfer the churned ice cream to a lidded container and freeze for at least 4 hours or until firm.

Serve the Chocolate Pistachio Ice Cream in bowls or cones, garnishing with extra roasted pistachios.

Enjoy this rich and nutty chocolate pistachio treat!

Include any tips for achieving a creamy texture and enhancing the pistachio flavor in your cookbook. This Chocolate Pistachio Ice Cream is a delightful and unique dessert that combines the richness of chocolate with the nuttiness of pistachios.

**Chocolate Hazelnut Cookies**

*Ingredients:*

- 1 cup unsalted butter, softened
- 1 cup granulated sugar
- 1 cup brown sugar, packed
- 2 large eggs
- 1 teaspoon vanilla extract
- 2 cups all-purpose flour
- 1/2 cup unsweetened cocoa powder
- 1 teaspoon baking soda
- 1/4 teaspoon salt
- 1 cup hazelnuts, toasted and finely chopped
- 1 cup semisweet chocolate chips or chunks

*Instructions:*

Preheat your oven to 350°F (175°C). Line baking sheets with parchment paper.
In a large bowl, cream together the softened butter, granulated sugar, and brown sugar until light and fluffy.
Add the eggs one at a time, beating well after each addition.
Stir in the vanilla extract.
In a separate bowl, whisk together the flour, cocoa powder, baking soda, and salt.
Gradually add the dry ingredients to the wet ingredients, mixing until just combined.
Fold in the finely chopped hazelnuts and semisweet chocolate chips or chunks.
Drop rounded tablespoons of dough onto the prepared baking sheets, spacing them about 2 inches apart.
Bake in the preheated oven for 10-12 minutes, or until the edges are set but the centers are still soft.
Allow the cookies to cool on the baking sheets for a few minutes before transferring them to a wire rack to cool completely.
Once cooled, store the Chocolate Hazelnut Cookies in an airtight container.
Serve and enjoy these delightful cookies with the perfect combination of chocolate and hazelnut flavors!

Feel free to customize the recipe by adding a drizzle of melted chocolate on top or sprinkling extra chopped hazelnuts for garnish. Include any tips for achieving a chewy or crispy texture in your cookbook. These Chocolate Hazelnut Cookies are a delightful treat for any occasion!

**Chocolate Raspberry Pancakes**

*Ingredients:*

- 1 cup all-purpose flour
- 2 tablespoons unsweetened cocoa powder
- 2 tablespoons granulated sugar
- 1 teaspoon baking powder
- 1/2 teaspoon baking soda
- 1/4 teaspoon salt
- 1 cup buttermilk
- 1 large egg
- 2 tablespoons unsalted butter, melted
- 1/2 cup fresh raspberries
- 1/2 cup semisweet chocolate chips
- Maple syrup for serving
- Additional raspberries for garnish

*Instructions:*

In a large mixing bowl, whisk together the flour, cocoa powder, sugar, baking powder, baking soda, and salt.
In a separate bowl, whisk together the buttermilk, egg, and melted butter.
Pour the wet ingredients into the dry ingredients and stir until just combined. The batter may be slightly lumpy.
Gently fold in the fresh raspberries and semisweet chocolate chips.
Heat a griddle or non-stick skillet over medium heat and lightly grease with cooking spray or butter.
Pour 1/4 cup of batter onto the griddle for each pancake.
Cook until bubbles form on the surface of the pancake, then flip and cook until the other side is golden brown.
Repeat until all the batter is used, adjusting heat if necessary to prevent burning.
Stack the Chocolate Raspberry Pancakes on a plate.
Serve the pancakes warm, drizzled with maple syrup, and garnished with additional raspberries.
Enjoy these delightful and indulgent pancakes with the perfect blend of chocolate and raspberries!

Feel free to customize the recipe by adding a dollop of whipped cream or a sprinkle of powdered sugar for extra sweetness. Include any tips for achieving fluffy and flavorful pancakes in your cookbook. These Chocolate Raspberry Pancakes are a delightful breakfast or brunch option!

**Chocolate Coconut Truffles**

*Ingredients:*

- 1 cup shredded coconut (plus extra for coating)
- 1/2 cup coconut cream
- 8 oz semisweet or dark chocolate, chopped
- 1 tablespoon coconut oil
- 1/2 teaspoon vanilla extract
- Pinch of salt

*Instructions:*

In a bowl, combine the shredded coconut, coconut cream, vanilla extract, and a pinch of salt. Mix until well combined.
Roll the coconut mixture into small truffle-sized balls and place them on a parchment paper-lined tray.
In a heatproof bowl, combine the chopped chocolate and coconut oil.
Melt the chocolate mixture using a double boiler or by microwaving in short intervals, stirring until smooth.
Dip each coconut ball into the melted chocolate, ensuring it is fully coated. Use a fork to lift the truffle out of the chocolate, allowing any excess to drip off.
Place the coated truffles back on the parchment paper-lined tray.
While the chocolate is still wet, sprinkle some additional shredded coconut on top of each truffle for decoration.
Repeat the process until all the coconut balls are coated and decorated.
Allow the chocolate to set by placing the tray in the refrigerator for at least 1-2 hours.
Once set, transfer the Chocolate Coconut Truffles to an airtight container and store them in the refrigerator.
Serve and enjoy these delightful and decadent truffles with the perfect combination of chocolate and coconut!

Feel free to experiment with different types of chocolate or add a hint of coconut extract for extra flavor. Include any tips for achieving a smooth chocolate coating and the ideal texture in your cookbook. These Chocolate Coconut Truffles are a delightful treat for coconut and chocolate enthusiasts!

**Chocolate Covered Banana Bites**

*Ingredients:*

- 3 large bananas, ripe but firm
- 8 oz semisweet or dark chocolate, chopped
- 2 tablespoons coconut oil
- Toppings of your choice (e.g., chopped nuts, shredded coconut, sprinkles)

*Instructions:*

Peel the bananas and cut them into bite-sized chunks.
Insert a toothpick or small skewer into each banana chunk. Place the bananas on a parchment paper-lined tray and freeze them for at least 1-2 hours.
In a heatproof bowl, combine the chopped chocolate and coconut oil.
Melt the chocolate mixture using a double boiler or by microwaving in short intervals, stirring until smooth.
Remove the frozen banana chunks from the freezer.
Dip each frozen banana chunk into the melted chocolate, ensuring it is fully coated. Use a fork to lift the banana out of the chocolate, allowing any excess to drip off.
Place the chocolate-covered banana bites back on the parchment paper-lined tray.
While the chocolate is still wet, sprinkle your choice of toppings on each banana bite.
Repeat the process until all banana bites are coated and decorated.
Place the tray back in the freezer for 15-20 minutes to allow the chocolate to set.
Once set, transfer the Chocolate Covered Banana Bites to an airtight container and store them in the freezer.
Serve and enjoy these delightful and refreshing treats with the perfect combination of chocolate and banana!

Feel free to get creative with the toppings or even drizzle additional melted chocolate on top. Include any tips for ensuring a smooth chocolate coating and preventing the banana bites from sticking together in your cookbook. These Chocolate Covered Banana Bites are a tasty and healthier dessert option!

**Chocolate Mint Ice Cream Sandwiches**

*Ingredients:*

For the Chocolate Cookies:

- 1 cup unsalted butter, softened
- 1 cup granulated sugar
- 1 large egg
- 1 teaspoon vanilla extract
- 2 cups all-purpose flour
- 1/2 cup unsweetened cocoa powder
- 1/2 teaspoon baking powder
- 1/4 teaspoon salt

For the Mint Chocolate Chip Ice Cream:

- 2 cups heavy cream
- 1 cup whole milk
- 3/4 cup granulated sugar
- 1 teaspoon peppermint extract
- Green food coloring (optional)
- 1 cup semisweet chocolate chips

*Instructions:*

For the Chocolate Cookies:

Preheat your oven to 350°F (175°C). Line baking sheets with parchment paper.
In a large bowl, cream together the softened butter and granulated sugar until light and fluffy.
Add the egg and vanilla extract, mixing until well combined.
In a separate bowl, whisk together the flour, cocoa powder, baking powder, and salt.
Gradually add the dry ingredients to the wet ingredients, mixing until a soft dough forms.

Divide the dough in half. Roll each half into a log about 2 inches in diameter. Wrap the logs in plastic wrap and refrigerate for at least 1 hour or until firm.
Slice the chilled logs into 1/4-inch thick rounds and place them on the prepared baking sheets.
Bake in the preheated oven for 10-12 minutes or until the edges are set.
Allow the cookies to cool on the baking sheets for a few minutes before transferring them to a wire rack to cool completely.

For the Mint Chocolate Chip Ice Cream:

In a medium saucepan, heat the heavy cream, whole milk, and granulated sugar over medium heat. Stir until the sugar is dissolved and the mixture is warm.
Remove from heat and stir in the peppermint extract. Add green food coloring if desired.
Allow the mixture to cool completely, then refrigerate for at least 4 hours or overnight.
Once chilled, churn the mint ice cream in an ice cream maker according to the manufacturer's instructions.
In the last few minutes of churning, add the semisweet chocolate chips.
Transfer the churned ice cream to a lidded container and freeze for at least 4 hours or until firm.

Assembly:

Once the cookies and ice cream are completely chilled and firm, scoop a generous amount of mint chocolate chip ice cream onto the bottom side of one cookie.
Place another cookie on top, pressing down slightly to form a sandwich.
Repeat the process until all sandwiches are assembled.
If desired, roll the sides of the ice cream sandwiches in additional chocolate chips or sprinkles.
Wrap each ice cream sandwich individually in plastic wrap and freeze until ready to serve.
Serve and enjoy these delightful Chocolate Mint Ice Cream Sandwiches!

Feel free to experiment with different cookie shapes or add extra mint flavoring to the ice cream. Include any tips for achieving the perfect cookie texture and ensuring the ice cream stays firm in your cookbook. These Chocolate Mint Ice Cream Sandwiches are a refreshing and indulgent treat!

**Chocolate Cherry Galette**

*Ingredients:*

For the Galette Dough:

- 1 1/4 cups all-purpose flour
- 1 tablespoon granulated sugar
- 1/4 teaspoon salt
- 1/2 cup unsalted butter, cold and cut into small pieces
- 3 to 4 tablespoons ice water

For the Chocolate Filling:

- 4 oz dark chocolate, chopped
- 2 tablespoons unsalted butter
- 2 tablespoons granulated sugar

For the Cherry Filling:

- 2 cups fresh cherries, pitted and halved
- 1/4 cup granulated sugar
- 1 tablespoon cornstarch
- 1 teaspoon vanilla extract

For Assembly:

- 1 egg (for egg wash)
- Coarse sugar for sprinkling (optional)

*Instructions:*

## For the Galette Dough:

In a food processor, combine the flour, sugar, and salt. Pulse to mix.

Add the cold, diced butter to the flour mixture. Pulse until the mixture resembles coarse crumbs.

With the food processor running, gradually add the ice water until the dough just comes together.

Turn the dough out onto a floured surface and shape it into a disk. Wrap it in plastic wrap and refrigerate for at least 1 hour.

## For the Chocolate Filling:

In a heatproof bowl, combine the chopped dark chocolate and butter.

Melt the chocolate and butter using a double boiler or by microwaving in short intervals, stirring until smooth.

Stir in the granulated sugar and set aside to cool.

## For the Cherry Filling:

In a bowl, toss the fresh cherry halves with sugar, cornstarch, and vanilla extract.

## Assembly:

Preheat your oven to 375°F (190°C). Line a baking sheet with parchment paper.

On a floured surface, roll out the chilled galette dough into a circle about 12 inches in diameter.

Transfer the rolled-out dough to the prepared baking sheet.

Spread the cooled chocolate filling over the center of the dough, leaving a border around the edges.

Arrange the cherry filling over the chocolate layer.

Fold the edges of the dough over the filling, creating a rustic border.

In a small bowl, beat the egg and brush it over the exposed edges of the galette.

Sprinkle coarse sugar over the egg-washed edges if desired.

Bake in the preheated oven for 30-35 minutes, or until the crust is golden brown.

Allow the Chocolate Cherry Galette to cool slightly before serving.

Serve and enjoy this delicious and visually appealing dessert!

Feel free to customize the galette by adding a scoop of vanilla ice cream or a dollop of whipped cream when serving. Include any tips for achieving a flaky crust and perfectly balanced flavors in your cookbook. This Chocolate Cherry Galette is a lovely and simple treat for any occasion!

**Chocolate Orange Biscotti**

*Ingredients:*

- 2 cups all-purpose flour
- 1/2 cup unsweetened cocoa powder
- 1 teaspoon baking powder
- 1/4 teaspoon salt
- 1/2 cup unsalted butter, softened
- 1 cup granulated sugar
- 2 large eggs
- 1 teaspoon vanilla extract
- Zest of 1 orange
- 1/2 cup semisweet chocolate chips or chunks
- 1/2 cup chopped almonds or hazelnuts

*For the Orange Glaze:*

- 1 cup powdered sugar
- 2 tablespoons fresh orange juice
- Zest of 1 orange

*Instructions:*

Preheat your oven to 350°F (175°C). Line a baking sheet with parchment paper.
In a bowl, whisk together the flour, cocoa powder, baking powder, and salt.
In another bowl, cream together the softened butter and granulated sugar until light and fluffy.

Add the eggs, one at a time, beating well after each addition. Stir in the vanilla extract and orange zest.

Gradually add the dry ingredients to the wet ingredients, mixing until just combined.

Fold in the semisweet chocolate chips or chunks and chopped nuts.

Divide the dough in half. On the prepared baking sheet, shape each half into a log about 12 inches long and 2 inches wide.

Bake in the preheated oven for 25-30 minutes, or until the logs are set.

Allow the logs to cool on the baking sheet for about 15 minutes. Reduce the oven temperature to 325°F (160°C).

Transfer the logs to a cutting board and slice them diagonally into 1/2-inch thick biscotti.

Place the biscotti back on the baking sheet, cut side down.

Bake for an additional 10-12 minutes, or until the biscotti are crisp and dry. Turn them over halfway through the baking time.

*For the Orange Glaze:*

In a bowl, whisk together the powdered sugar, fresh orange juice, and orange zest until smooth.

Once the biscotti have cooled, drizzle the orange glaze over the top.

Allow the glaze to set before serving.

Serve and enjoy these delightful Chocolate Orange Biscotti with a cup of coffee or tea!

Feel free to customize the recipe by adding more orange zest for a stronger citrus flavor or dipping the biscotti in melted chocolate. Include any tips for achieving the perfect crunch and flavor balance in your cookbook. These Chocolate Orange Biscotti make a lovely accompaniment to your hot beverage!

**Chocolate Strawberry Tartlets**

*Ingredients:*

For the Tartlet Shells:

- 1 1/4 cups all-purpose flour
- 1/4 cup unsweetened cocoa powder
- 1/2 cup unsalted butter, cold and cut into small pieces
- 1/4 cup granulated sugar
- 1 large egg yolk
- 2 tablespoons ice water

For the Chocolate Ganache:

- 8 oz semisweet chocolate, chopped
- 1 cup heavy cream

For the Strawberry Topping:

- 1 pint fresh strawberries, hulled and sliced
- 1/4 cup strawberry jam, melted

*Instructions:*

For the Tartlet Shells:

>In a food processor, combine the flour, cocoa powder, and granulated sugar. Pulse to mix.

Add the cold, diced butter to the flour mixture. Pulse until the mixture resembles coarse crumbs.

In a small bowl, whisk together the egg yolk and ice water.

With the food processor running, gradually add the egg yolk mixture until the dough just comes together.

Turn the dough out onto a floured surface and shape it into a disk. Wrap it in plastic wrap and refrigerate for at least 30 minutes.

Preheat your oven to 375°F (190°C).

Roll out the chilled dough on a floured surface to about 1/8-inch thickness.

Cut the dough into circles to fit your tartlet pans.

Press the dough into the tartlet pans, trimming any excess.

Prick the bottom of the tartlet shells with a fork.

Bake in the preheated oven for 12-15 minutes or until the shells are set. Allow them to cool completely.

For the Chocolate Ganache:

Place the chopped semisweet chocolate in a heatproof bowl.

In a saucepan, heat the heavy cream until it just begins to simmer.

Pour the hot cream over the chocolate and let it sit for a minute.

Stir the mixture until the chocolate is completely melted and the ganache is smooth.

Allow the ganache to cool slightly.

Pour the chocolate ganache into the cooled tartlet shells, spreading it evenly.

For the Strawberry Topping:

Arrange the sliced strawberries over the chocolate ganache in an attractive pattern.

Brush the melted strawberry jam over the top of the strawberries for a glossy finish.

Refrigerate the tartlets for at least 1-2 hours to allow the chocolate ganache to set.

Serve and enjoy these elegant Chocolate Strawberry Tartlets!

Feel free to customize the tartlets by adding a sprinkle of powdered sugar or garnishing with fresh mint leaves. Include any tips for achieving a perfect crust and creating a visually appealing presentation in your cookbook. These Chocolate Strawberry Tartlets are a delightful and decadent dessert for any occasion!

**Chocolate Almond Butter Cups**

*Ingredients:*

- 1 cup semisweet or dark chocolate chips
- 1 tablespoon coconut oil
- 1/2 cup almond butter (homemade or store-bought)
- 2 tablespoons powdered sugar
- 1/2 teaspoon vanilla extract
- Pinch of salt
- Sliced almonds for garnish (optional)

*Instructions:*

Line a mini muffin tin with paper or silicone cupcake liners.

In a microwave-safe bowl, combine the chocolate chips and coconut oil.

Microwave the chocolate mixture in 20-30 second intervals, stirring between each interval, until the chocolate is completely melted and smooth.

Spoon a small amount of melted chocolate into the bottom of each cupcake liner, ensuring it covers the base.

Place the muffin tin in the freezer for about 10 minutes to set the chocolate.

In a bowl, mix together the almond butter, powdered sugar, vanilla extract, and a pinch of salt until well combined.

Remove the muffin tin from the freezer and place a small spoonful of the almond butter mixture on top of the hardened chocolate layer in each cup.

Flatten the almond butter layer slightly with the back of a spoon.

Spoon the remaining melted chocolate over the almond butter, covering it completely.

If desired, garnish each almond butter cup with sliced almonds.

Return the muffin tin to the freezer for an additional 20-30 minutes, or until the chocolate is fully set.

Once set, remove the Chocolate Almond Butter Cups from the muffin tin.

Store the cups in the refrigerator until ready to serve.

Serve and enjoy these delightful and nutty Chocolate Almond Butter Cups!

Feel free to experiment with different nut butters or add a sprinkle of sea salt on top for extra flavor. Include any tips for achieving a smooth chocolate coating and ensuring the almond butter stays firm in your cookbook. These Chocolate Almond Butter Cups are a delicious and healthier alternative to store-bought treats!

**Chocolate Coconut Chia Pudding**

*Ingredients:*

- 1/4 cup chia seeds
- 1 cup coconut milk (canned or homemade)
- 2 tablespoons unsweetened cocoa powder
- 2-3 tablespoons maple syrup or sweetener of your choice
- 1/2 teaspoon vanilla extract
- Shredded coconut and chocolate shavings for garnish (optional)
- Fresh berries for topping (optional)

*Instructions:*

In a bowl, whisk together the chia seeds, coconut milk, cocoa powder, maple syrup, and vanilla extract.

Continue whisking for a few minutes to ensure the cocoa powder is fully incorporated and there are no lumps.

Cover the bowl and refrigerate the mixture for at least 4 hours or overnight. Stir the mixture once or twice during the initial hour to prevent clumping.

After refrigeration, the chia seeds will absorb the liquid and create a pudding-like consistency.

Before serving, give the Chocolate Coconut Chia Pudding a good stir to ensure an even texture.

Spoon the pudding into serving glasses or bowls.

Garnish with shredded coconut, chocolate shavings, and fresh berries if desired.

Serve and enjoy this delicious and nutritious Chocolate Coconut Chia Pudding!

Feel free to customize the recipe by adding sliced almonds, chopped nuts, or a dollop of coconut whipped cream on top. Include any tips for achieving the desired thickness and sweetness in your cookbook. This Chocolate Coconut Chia Pudding is a delightful and guilt-free dessert or breakfast option!

**Chocolate Walnut Blondies**

*Ingredients:*

- 1 cup (2 sticks) unsalted butter, melted
- 2 cups light brown sugar, packed
- 2 large eggs
- 1 teaspoon vanilla extract
- 2 cups all-purpose flour
- 1/2 teaspoon baking powder
- 1/4 teaspoon baking soda
- 1/2 teaspoon salt
- 1 cup semisweet chocolate chips
- 1 cup chopped walnuts

*Instructions:*

Preheat your oven to 350°F (175°C). Grease a 9x13-inch baking pan and line it with parchment paper, leaving an overhang on two sides.

In a large bowl, whisk together the melted butter and brown sugar until well combined.

Add the eggs and vanilla extract to the butter-sugar mixture, whisking until smooth.

In a separate bowl, whisk together the flour, baking powder, baking soda, and salt.

Gradually add the dry ingredients to the wet ingredients, stirring until just combined.

Fold in the chocolate chips and chopped walnuts, ensuring they are evenly distributed throughout the batter.

Pour the batter into the prepared baking pan, spreading it evenly.

Bake in the preheated oven for 25-30 minutes or until a toothpick inserted into the center comes out with moist crumbs (not wet batter).

Allow the Blondies to cool completely in the pan on a wire rack.

Once cooled, use the parchment overhang to lift the Blondies out of the pan. Place them on a cutting board.

Cut the Blondies into squares or rectangles of your desired size.

Serve and enjoy these delicious Chocolate Walnut Blondies!

Feel free to add a sprinkle of sea salt on top for a sweet-savory contrast or drizzle with melted chocolate for an extra touch. Include any tips for achieving a chewy and moist texture in your cookbook. These Chocolate Walnut Blondies are a delightful treat for chocolate and nut lovers!

**Chocolate Raspberry Bread Pudding**

*Ingredients:*

- 8 cups cubed day-old bread (such as French or Italian bread)
- 1 cup fresh raspberries
- 1 cup semisweet chocolate chips
- 4 large eggs
- 2 cups whole milk
- 1 cup heavy cream
- 1 cup granulated sugar
- 1 teaspoon vanilla extract
- 1/2 teaspoon cinnamon
- Pinch of salt
- Powdered sugar for dusting (optional)
- Whipped cream for serving (optional)

*Instructions:*

Preheat your oven to 350°F (175°C). Grease a 9x13-inch baking dish.

In a large bowl, combine the cubed bread, fresh raspberries, and semisweet chocolate chips. Toss to mix evenly.

In another bowl, whisk together the eggs, whole milk, heavy cream, granulated sugar, vanilla extract, cinnamon, and a pinch of salt.

Pour the egg mixture over the bread mixture, making sure to coat all the bread evenly. Allow it to soak for about 15-20 minutes, pressing down on the bread occasionally to ensure absorption.

Transfer the soaked bread mixture to the prepared baking dish, spreading it evenly.

Bake in the preheated oven for 45-50 minutes or until the top is golden brown and the center is set.

Remove the Chocolate Raspberry Bread Pudding from the oven and let it cool slightly.

If desired, dust the top with powdered sugar before serving.

Serve warm, optionally topped with a dollop of whipped cream.

Enjoy this decadent Chocolate Raspberry Bread Pudding!

Feel free to customize the recipe by adding a raspberry or chocolate drizzle on top. Include any tips for achieving the perfect balance of sweetness and texture in your cookbook. This Chocolate Raspberry Bread Pudding is a delightful dessert for any occasion!

**Chocolate Walnut Blondies**

*Ingredients:*

- 1 cup (2 sticks) unsalted butter, melted
- 2 cups light brown sugar, packed
- 2 large eggs
- 1 teaspoon vanilla extract
- 2 cups all-purpose flour
- 1/2 teaspoon baking powder
- 1/4 teaspoon baking soda
- 1/2 teaspoon salt
- 1 cup semisweet chocolate chips
- 1 cup chopped walnuts

*Instructions:*

Preheat your oven to 350°F (175°C). Grease a 9x13-inch baking pan and line it with parchment paper, leaving an overhang on two sides.

In a large bowl, whisk together the melted butter and brown sugar until well combined.

Add the eggs and vanilla extract to the butter-sugar mixture, whisking until smooth.

In a separate bowl, whisk together the flour, baking powder, baking soda, and salt.

Gradually add the dry ingredients to the wet ingredients, stirring until just combined.

Fold in the chocolate chips and chopped walnuts, ensuring they are evenly distributed throughout the batter.

Pour the batter into the prepared baking pan, spreading it evenly.

Bake in the preheated oven for 25-30 minutes or until a toothpick inserted into the center comes out with moist crumbs (not wet batter).

Allow the Blondies to cool completely in the pan on a wire rack.

Once cooled, use the parchment overhang to lift the Blondies out of the pan. Place them on a cutting board.

Cut the Blondies into squares or rectangles of your desired size.

Serve and enjoy these delicious Chocolate Walnut Blondies!

Feel free to add a sprinkle of sea salt on top for a sweet-savory contrast or drizzle with melted chocolate for an extra touch. Include any tips for achieving a chewy and moist texture in your cookbook. These Chocolate Walnut Blondies are a delightful treat for chocolate and nut lovers!

**Chocolate Raspberry Bread Pudding**

*Ingredients:*

- 8 cups cubed day-old bread (such as French or Italian bread)
- 1 cup fresh raspberries
- 1 cup semisweet chocolate chips
- 4 large eggs
- 2 cups whole milk
- 1 cup heavy cream
- 1 cup granulated sugar
- 1 teaspoon vanilla extract
- 1/2 teaspoon cinnamon
- Pinch of salt
- Powdered sugar for dusting (optional)
- Whipped cream for serving (optional)

*Instructions:*

Preheat your oven to 350°F (175°C). Grease a 9x13-inch baking dish.

In a large bowl, combine the cubed bread, fresh raspberries, and semisweet chocolate chips. Toss to mix evenly.

In another bowl, whisk together the eggs, whole milk, heavy cream, granulated sugar, vanilla extract, cinnamon, and a pinch of salt.

Pour the egg mixture over the bread mixture, making sure to coat all the bread evenly. Allow it to soak for about 15-20 minutes, pressing down on the bread occasionally to ensure absorption.

Transfer the soaked bread mixture to the prepared baking dish, spreading it evenly.

Bake in the preheated oven for 45-50 minutes or until the top is golden brown and the center is set.

Remove the Chocolate Raspberry Bread Pudding from the oven and let it cool slightly.

If desired, dust the top with powdered sugar before serving.

Serve warm, optionally topped with a dollop of whipped cream.

Enjoy this decadent Chocolate Raspberry Bread Pudding!

Feel free to customize the recipe by adding a raspberry or chocolate drizzle on top. Include any tips for achieving the perfect balance of sweetness and texture in your cookbook. This Chocolate Raspberry Bread Pudding is a delightful dessert for any occasion!

**Chocolate Caramel Pretzel Bars**

*Ingredients:*

For the Pretzel Crust:

- 2 cups pretzel crumbs (about 8 oz pretzels, crushed)
- 3/4 cup unsalted butter, melted
- 1/4 cup granulated sugar

For the Caramel Layer:

- 1 cup unsalted butter
- 1 cup packed brown sugar
- 1/2 cup light corn syrup
- 1/2 teaspoon salt
- 1 can (14 oz) sweetened condensed milk

For the Chocolate Topping:

- 2 cups semisweet chocolate chips
- 1/2 cup creamy peanut butter (optional, for a smoother chocolate layer)
- Crushed pretzels for garnish (optional)

*Instructions:*

For the Pretzel Crust:

Preheat your oven to 350°F (175°C). Line a 9x13-inch baking dish with parchment paper, leaving an overhang on two sides.

In a bowl, combine the pretzel crumbs, melted butter, and granulated sugar. Mix until the crumbs are well coated.

Press the pretzel mixture firmly into the bottom of the prepared baking dish.

Bake the crust in the preheated oven for about 8-10 minutes or until set. Allow it to cool while preparing the caramel layer.

For the Caramel Layer:

In a saucepan over medium heat, melt the butter for the caramel layer.

Stir in the brown sugar, light corn syrup, and salt. Cook, stirring constantly, until the mixture comes to a boil.

Once boiling, add the sweetened condensed milk and continue to cook, stirring constantly, for about 5-7 minutes or until the caramel thickens.

Pour the caramel over the cooled pretzel crust, spreading it evenly.

For the Chocolate Topping:

In a microwave-safe bowl, melt the semisweet chocolate chips (and peanut butter if using) in 20-30 second intervals, stirring between each interval until smooth.

Pour the melted chocolate over the caramel layer, spreading it evenly.

If desired, sprinkle crushed pretzels on top for added texture.

Allow the bars to cool completely in the refrigerator for at least 2 hours or until the chocolate is set.

Once set, use the parchment overhang to lift the bars out of the baking dish. Place them on a cutting board.

Cut into squares or bars of your desired size.

Serve and enjoy these delicious Chocolate Caramel Pretzel Bars!

Feel free to experiment with different types of pretzels or drizzle additional caramel on top for extra indulgence. Include any tips for achieving the perfect balance of sweet, salty, and crunchy in your cookbook. These Chocolate Caramel Pretzel Bars are a delightful and addictive treat!

# Chocolate Peanut Butter Banana Smoothie

*Ingredients:*

- 2 ripe bananas, peeled and sliced
- 1 cup milk (dairy or plant-based)
- 1/4 cup creamy peanut butter
- 2 tablespoons unsweetened cocoa powder
- 1 tablespoon honey or maple syrup (optional, depending on sweetness preference)
- 1/2 teaspoon vanilla extract
- 1 cup ice cubes

*Instructions:*

In a blender, combine the sliced bananas, milk, creamy peanut butter, unsweetened cocoa powder, honey or maple syrup (if using), vanilla extract, and ice cubes.

Blend on high speed until all ingredients are well combined and the smoothie reaches a creamy consistency.

Taste the smoothie and adjust sweetness if necessary by adding more honey or maple syrup.

Continue blending until the ice is completely crushed and the smoothie is smooth and creamy.

Pour the Chocolate Peanut Butter Banana Smoothie into glasses.

If desired, garnish with a drizzle of peanut butter or a sprinkle of cocoa powder.

Serve immediately and enjoy this delicious and satisfying smoothie!

Feel free to customize the recipe by adding a handful of spinach for a nutrient boost or incorporating protein powder for an extra protein kick. Include any tips for achieving the perfect thickness and flavor balance in your cookbook. This Chocolate Peanut Butter Banana Smoothie is a delightful and nutritious beverage for a quick and tasty treat!

**Chocolate Toffee Cheesecake**

*Ingredients:*

For the Crust:

- 1 1/2 cups chocolate cookie crumbs
- 1/3 cup unsalted butter, melted
- 1/4 cup granulated sugar

For the Cheesecake Filling:

- 24 oz cream cheese, softened
- 1 cup granulated sugar
- 3 large eggs
- 1 cup sour cream
- 1 teaspoon vanilla extract
- 1/2 cup toffee bits (plus extra for garnish)

For the Chocolate Ganache:

- 1 cup semisweet chocolate chips
- 1/2 cup heavy cream
- 2 tablespoons unsalted butter

*Instructions:*

For the Crust:

    Preheat your oven to 325°F (163°C). Grease a 9-inch springform pan.

In a bowl, combine the chocolate cookie crumbs, melted butter, and granulated sugar. Mix until the crumbs are well coated.

Press the mixture firmly into the bottom of the prepared springform pan to form the crust.

Bake the crust in the preheated oven for 10 minutes. Allow it to cool while preparing the cheesecake filling.

For the Cheesecake Filling:

In a large mixing bowl, beat the softened cream cheese until smooth.

Add the granulated sugar and continue to beat until well combined.

Add the eggs, one at a time, beating well after each addition.

Mix in the sour cream and vanilla extract until the batter is smooth and creamy.

Fold in the toffee bits until evenly distributed throughout the batter.

Pour the cheesecake filling over the cooled crust in the springform pan, spreading it evenly.

Bake in the preheated oven for 55-60 minutes or until the edges are set, and the center is slightly jiggly.

Turn off the oven and let the cheesecake cool in the oven for 1 hour.

Remove the cheesecake from the oven and refrigerate for at least 4 hours or overnight to chill.

For the Chocolate Ganache:

In a heatproof bowl, combine the semisweet chocolate chips, heavy cream, and butter.

Heat the mixture in the microwave or on the stovetop until the chocolate is melted. Stir until smooth.

Allow the ganache to cool slightly.

Pour the chocolate ganache over the chilled cheesecake, spreading it evenly.

Garnish with additional toffee bits.

Return the cheesecake to the refrigerator to allow the ganache to set.

Once set, remove the sides of the springform pan.

Slice and serve this decadent Chocolate Toffee Cheesecake!

Feel free to customize the recipe by adding a caramel drizzle or chopped nuts. Include any tips for achieving a smooth and creamy texture in your cookbook. This Chocolate Toffee Cheesecake is a delightful and indulgent dessert for any occasion!

**Chocolate Hazelnut Croissants**

*Ingredients:*

- 1 sheet of puff pastry (store-bought or homemade)
- 1/2 cup chocolate hazelnut spread (such as Nutella)
- 1/4 cup chopped hazelnuts
- 1 egg, beaten (for egg wash)
- Powdered sugar for dusting (optional)

*Instructions:*

Preheat your oven to the temperature recommended on the puff pastry package or recipe.

Roll out the puff pastry sheet on a lightly floured surface into a rectangle.

Spread the chocolate hazelnut spread evenly over the entire surface of the puff pastry.

Sprinkle the chopped hazelnuts over the chocolate hazelnut spread.

Starting from one of the longer sides, tightly roll the puff pastry into a log.

Using a sharp knife, slice the log into individual croissants, about 1 to 1.5 inches thick.

Place the croissants on a baking sheet lined with parchment paper, leaving some space between each.

Brush the tops of the croissants with the beaten egg to give them a shiny finish.

Bake in the preheated oven according to the puff pastry package or recipe instructions, usually until golden brown and puffed.

Once baked, remove the chocolate hazelnut croissants from the oven and allow them to cool slightly.

Optionally, dust the croissants with powdered sugar before serving.

Serve and enjoy these delightful Chocolate Hazelnut Croissants with your favorite hot beverage!

Feel free to customize the recipe by adding a drizzle of melted chocolate on top or incorporating finely chopped dark chocolate into the hazelnut spread. Include any tips for achieving a flaky and buttery texture in your cookbook. These Chocolate Hazelnut Croissants make for a delicious breakfast or indulgent treat!

**Chocolate Raspberry Chia Seed Pudding**

*Ingredients:*

- 1/4 cup chia seeds
- 1 cup milk (dairy or plant-based)
- 2 tablespoons unsweetened cocoa powder
- 2 tablespoons maple syrup or sweetener of your choice
- 1/2 teaspoon vanilla extract
- 1/2 cup fresh raspberries
- Chocolate shavings for garnish (optional)

*Instructions:*

In a bowl, whisk together the chia seeds, milk, cocoa powder, maple syrup, and vanilla extract.

Stir the mixture well to ensure the cocoa powder is fully incorporated and there are no lumps.

Cover the bowl and refrigerate the mixture for at least 4 hours or overnight. Stir the mixture once or twice during the initial hour to prevent clumping.

After refrigeration, the chia seeds will absorb the liquid and create a pudding-like consistency.

Before serving, give the Chocolate Raspberry Chia Seed Pudding a good stir to ensure an even texture.

Spoon the pudding into serving glasses or bowls.

Top the pudding with fresh raspberries and, if desired, chocolate shavings for garnish.

Serve and enjoy this delightful and nutritious Chocolate Raspberry Chia Seed Pudding!

Feel free to customize the recipe by adding a drizzle of raspberry sauce or incorporating sliced almonds for added crunch. Include any tips for achieving the desired thickness and sweetness in your cookbook. This Chocolate Raspberry Chia Seed Pudding is a tasty and healthy dessert or breakfast option!

**Chocolate Mint Cheesecake**

*Ingredients:*

For the Crust:

- 1 1/2 cups chocolate cookie crumbs
- 1/3 cup unsalted butter, melted
- 1/4 cup granulated sugar

For the Cheesecake Filling:

- 24 oz cream cheese, softened
- 1 cup granulated sugar
- 3 large eggs
- 1 cup sour cream
- 1 teaspoon peppermint extract
- Green food coloring (optional)
- 1/2 cup chocolate chips (semisweet or dark)

For the Chocolate Ganache:

- 1 cup semisweet chocolate chips
- 1/2 cup heavy cream
- 2 tablespoons unsalted butter
- Crushed mint candies for garnish (optional)

*Instructions:*

For the Crust:

> Preheat your oven to 325°F (163°C). Grease a 9-inch springform pan.
>
> In a bowl, combine the chocolate cookie crumbs, melted butter, and granulated sugar. Mix until the crumbs are well coated.
>
> Press the mixture firmly into the bottom of the prepared springform pan to form the crust.
>
> Bake the crust in the preheated oven for 10 minutes. Allow it to cool while preparing the cheesecake filling.

For the Cheesecake Filling:

> In a large mixing bowl, beat the softened cream cheese until smooth.
>
> Add the granulated sugar and continue to beat until well combined.
>
> Add the eggs, one at a time, beating well after each addition.
>
> Mix in the sour cream, peppermint extract, and green food coloring (if using) until the batter is smooth.
>
> Fold in the chocolate chips until evenly distributed throughout the batter.
>
> Pour the cheesecake filling over the cooled crust in the springform pan, spreading it evenly.
>
> Bake in the preheated oven for 55-60 minutes or until the edges are set, and the center is slightly jiggly.
>
> Turn off the oven and let the cheesecake cool in the oven for 1 hour.
>
> Remove the cheesecake from the oven and refrigerate for at least 4 hours or overnight to chill.

For the Chocolate Ganache:

In a heatproof bowl, combine the semisweet chocolate chips, heavy cream, and butter.

Heat the mixture in the microwave or on the stovetop until the chocolate is melted. Stir until smooth.

Allow the ganache to cool slightly.

Pour the chocolate ganache over the chilled cheesecake, spreading it evenly.

Garnish with crushed mint candies if desired.

Return the cheesecake to the refrigerator to allow the ganache to set.

Once set, remove the sides of the springform pan.

Slice and serve this decadent Chocolate Mint Cheesecake!

Feel free to customize the recipe by adding a layer of mint whipped cream or a sprinkle of cocoa powder on top. Include any tips for achieving a smooth and creamy texture in your cookbook. This Chocolate Mint Cheesecake is a delightful and festive dessert for mint chocolate lovers!

**Chocolate Almond Flourless Cake**

*Ingredients:*

- 1 cup (2 sticks) unsalted butter
- 1 cup granulated sugar
- 1 cup semisweet or dark chocolate chips
- 1 cup almond flour
- 1/4 teaspoon salt
- 4 large eggs
- 1 teaspoon vanilla extract
- Powdered sugar for dusting (optional)
- Sliced almonds for garnish (optional)

*Instructions:*

Preheat your oven to 350°F (175°C). Grease a 9-inch round cake pan and line the bottom with parchment paper.

In a saucepan over medium heat, melt the butter and sugar together, stirring until well combined.

Add the chocolate chips to the melted butter and sugar mixture. Stir until the chocolate is completely melted and smooth. Remove from heat.

Allow the chocolate mixture to cool slightly.

In a bowl, whisk together the almond flour and salt.

Add the almond flour mixture to the melted chocolate mixture, stirring until well combined.

In a separate bowl, beat the eggs and vanilla extract together.

Gradually add the beaten eggs to the chocolate-almond mixture, stirring until smooth.

Pour the batter into the prepared cake pan, spreading it evenly.

Bake in the preheated oven for approximately 25-30 minutes or until a toothpick inserted into the center comes out with moist crumbs (not wet batter).

Allow the flourless cake to cool in the pan for about 10 minutes, then transfer it to a wire rack to cool completely.

Once cooled, dust the top with powdered sugar and garnish with sliced almonds if desired.

Slice and serve this rich and decadent Chocolate Almond Flourless Cake!

Feel free to serve it with a dollop of whipped cream or a scoop of vanilla ice cream for an extra treat. Include any tips for achieving a moist and fudgy texture in your cookbook. This Chocolate Almond Flourless Cake is a delightful gluten-free option for chocolate enthusiasts!

**Chocolate Cherry Clafoutis**

*Ingredients:*

- 1 cup fresh cherries, pitted and halved
- 1/2 cup semisweet chocolate chips or chopped chocolate
- 3/4 cup all-purpose flour
- 1/2 cup granulated sugar
- Pinch of salt
- 3 large eggs
- 1 cup milk (dairy or plant-based)
- 1 teaspoon vanilla extract
- Powdered sugar for dusting (optional)

*Instructions:*

Preheat your oven to 350°F (175°C). Grease a baking dish or tart pan.

Scatter the pitted and halved cherries, as well as the chocolate chips, evenly in the bottom of the prepared pan.

In a bowl, whisk together the flour, granulated sugar, and a pinch of salt.

In a separate bowl, whisk together the eggs, milk, and vanilla extract.

Gradually add the wet ingredients to the dry ingredients, whisking until you have a smooth batter.

Pour the batter over the cherries and chocolate in the baking dish.

Bake in the preheated oven for about 35-40 minutes or until the clafoutis is set and golden brown on top.

Remove from the oven and let it cool slightly.

Dust the top with powdered sugar if desired.

Slice and serve this delightful Chocolate Cherry Clafoutis warm.

Feel free to serve it with a scoop of vanilla ice cream or a dollop of whipped cream for an extra touch. Include any tips for achieving the perfect balance of sweetness and texture in your cookbook. This Chocolate Cherry Clafoutis is a classic French dessert with a chocolatey twist!

**Chocolate Orange Scones**

*Ingredients:*

- 2 cups all-purpose flour
- 1/4 cup granulated sugar
- 1 tablespoon baking powder
- 1/2 teaspoon salt
- 1/2 cup unsalted butter, cold and cut into small cubes
- 1/2 cup semisweet chocolate chips or chopped chocolate
- Zest of 1 orange
- 2/3 cup milk (dairy or plant-based)
- 1 teaspoon vanilla extract
- 1 tablespoon fresh orange juice

*For the Glaze:*

- 1 cup powdered sugar
- 2 tablespoons fresh orange juice
- Zest of 1 orange

*Instructions:*

Preheat your oven to 425°F (220°C). Line a baking sheet with parchment paper.
In a large bowl, whisk together the flour, sugar, baking powder, and salt.
Add the cold, cubed butter to the dry ingredients. Use a pastry cutter or your fingers to cut the butter into the flour until the mixture resembles coarse crumbs.
Stir in the chocolate chips and orange zest.

In a separate bowl, combine the milk, vanilla extract, and fresh orange juice. Gradually add the wet ingredients to the dry ingredients, stirring until just combined. Be careful not to overmix.

Turn the dough out onto a floured surface and gently knead it a few times until it comes together.

Pat the dough into a circle about 1 inch thick.

Use a round cutter or a sharp knife to cut out scones from the dough. Place the scones on the prepared baking sheet.

Bake in the preheated oven for 12-15 minutes or until the scones are golden brown.

While the scones are baking, prepare the glaze. In a bowl, whisk together the powdered sugar, fresh orange juice, and orange zest until smooth.

Once the scones are done baking, let them cool on a wire rack for a few minutes. Drizzle the glaze over the warm scones.

Serve and enjoy these delightful Chocolate Orange Scones with a cup of tea or coffee!

Include any tips for achieving flaky and tender scones in your cookbook. These Chocolate Orange Scones are a perfect blend of citrusy and chocolatey flavors!

**Chocolate Raspberry Crepes**

*Ingredients:*

For the Crepes:

- 1 cup all-purpose flour
- 2 tablespoons unsweetened cocoa powder
- 2 tablespoons granulated sugar
- 1/4 teaspoon salt
- 3 large eggs
- 1 1/2 cups milk (dairy or plant-based)
- 2 tablespoons unsalted butter, melted
- 1 teaspoon vanilla extract

For the Filling:

- 1 cup fresh raspberries
- 1/2 cup chocolate chips or chopped chocolate
- Whipped cream for serving
- Powdered sugar for dusting

*Instructions:*

For the Crepes:

> In a blender, combine the flour, cocoa powder, sugar, salt, eggs, milk, melted butter, and vanilla extract. Blend until smooth.

Let the crepe batter rest for at least 30 minutes in the refrigerator to allow the flour to absorb the liquid.

Heat a non-stick skillet or crepe pan over medium heat. Lightly grease with butter or cooking spray.

Pour a small amount of batter into the center of the pan, swirling to spread it thinly across the bottom.

Cook for about 1-2 minutes until the edges begin to lift. Flip the crepe and cook for an additional 30 seconds to 1 minute on the other side.

Repeat until all the batter is used, stacking the crepes on a plate as you go.

Assembly:

Lay a crepe flat on a serving plate.

Spread a handful of fresh raspberries and a sprinkle of chocolate chips over one-half of the crepe.

Fold the crepe in half over the filling and then fold it in half again to form a triangle.

Continue assembling the remaining crepes.

Top the folded crepes with a dollop of whipped cream.

Dust with powdered sugar just before serving.

Serve and enjoy these delectable Chocolate Raspberry Crepes as a delightful dessert or breakfast treat!

Feel free to drizzle with additional melted chocolate or garnish with mint leaves for extra flair. Include any tips for achieving thin and delicate crepes in your cookbook. These Chocolate Raspberry Crepes are a delightful and elegant dish for any occasion!

# Chocolate Peanut Butter Energy Bites

*Ingredients:*

- 1 cup old-fashioned oats
- 1/2 cup creamy peanut butter
- 1/3 cup honey or maple syrup
- 1/2 cup ground flaxseed
- 1/2 cup chocolate chips
- 1 teaspoon vanilla extract
- A pinch of salt

*Instructions:*

In a large mixing bowl, combine the old-fashioned oats, creamy peanut butter, honey or maple syrup, ground flaxseed, chocolate chips, vanilla extract, and a pinch of salt.

Stir the ingredients until well combined.

Place the mixture in the refrigerator for about 30 minutes to firm up.

Once chilled, use your hands to roll the mixture into bite-sized balls. You can adjust the size based on your preference.

Arrange the Chocolate Peanut Butter Energy Bites on a plate or tray.

Refrigerate the energy bites for an additional 15-30 minutes to set.

Store the energy bites in an airtight container in the refrigerator for freshness.

Serve and enjoy these delicious and nutritious Chocolate Peanut Butter Energy Bites as a quick snack or energy boost!

Feel free to customize the recipe by adding ingredients like chopped nuts, chia seeds, or dried fruits. Include any tips for shaping the bites and storing them to maintain freshness in your cookbook. These Chocolate Peanut Butter Energy Bites are a convenient and tasty snack for those on the go!

**Chocolate Covered Blueberries**

*Ingredients:*

- 1 cup fresh blueberries, washed and dried
- 1/2 cup dark chocolate chips or chopped dark chocolate
- 1 teaspoon coconut oil (optional)
- White chocolate for drizzling (optional)

*Instructions:*

Line a baking sheet with parchment paper.

In a microwave-safe bowl, melt the dark chocolate chips (or chopped chocolate) in 20-30 second intervals, stirring between each interval. Add coconut oil if needed to achieve a smoother consistency.

Once the chocolate is melted and smooth, dip each blueberry into the chocolate, making sure it is evenly coated.

Using a fork, lift the chocolate-coated blueberry, allowing any excess chocolate to drip off.

Place the chocolate-covered blueberries on the prepared baking sheet, ensuring they are not touching each other.

If desired, melt white chocolate and drizzle it over the chocolate-covered blueberries for an extra decorative touch.

Allow the chocolate to set. You can place the baking sheet in the refrigerator for quicker setting.

Once set, transfer the Chocolate Covered Blueberries to a serving plate or store in an airtight container.

Serve and enjoy these delicious and elegant Chocolate Covered Blueberries as a sweet treat or dessert!

Feel free to experiment with different types of chocolate or add a sprinkle of sea salt for flavor contrast. Include any tips for achieving a smooth chocolate coating and preventing the blueberries from clumping in your cookbook. These Chocolate Covered Blueberries make for a delightful and healthier indulgence!

**Chocolate Pecan Caramel Rolls**

*Ingredients:*

For the Dough:

- 1 package (2 1/4 teaspoons) active dry yeast
- 1 cup warm milk (110°F/43°C)
- 1/4 cup granulated sugar
- 1/4 cup unsalted butter, melted
- 1 teaspoon salt
- 2 large eggs
- 4 cups all-purpose flour

For the Filling:

- 1/2 cup unsalted butter, softened
- 1 cup brown sugar, packed
- 2 tablespoons unsweetened cocoa powder
- 1 cup chopped pecans

For the Caramel Sauce:

- 1 cup unsalted butter
- 1 cup brown sugar, packed
- 1/2 cup heavy cream
- 1 teaspoon vanilla extract
- A pinch of salt

*Instructions:*

For the Dough:

In a bowl, dissolve the yeast in warm milk and let it sit for about 5 minutes until it becomes frothy.

In a large mixing bowl, combine the yeast mixture, sugar, melted butter, salt, and eggs.

Gradually add the flour, one cup at a time, stirring well after each addition.

Knead the dough on a floured surface until smooth and elastic, about 5-7 minutes.

Place the dough in a greased bowl, cover it with a kitchen towel, and let it rise in a warm place for 1-2 hours or until it doubles in size.

For the Filling:

In a bowl, mix together the softened butter, brown sugar, cocoa powder, and chopped pecans until well combined.

For the Caramel Sauce:

In a saucepan over medium heat, melt the butter.

Stir in the brown sugar, heavy cream, vanilla extract, and a pinch of salt.

Bring the mixture to a boil, stirring constantly, and let it boil for 2-3 minutes until slightly thickened.

Remove the caramel sauce from heat and let it cool slightly.

Assembly:

Preheat your oven to 350°F (175°C). Grease a baking dish.

Roll out the risen dough on a floured surface into a large rectangle.

Spread the filling mixture evenly over the dough.

Roll the dough into a log and cut it into slices, about 1-2 inches thick.

Place the slices in the greased baking dish.

Pour the caramel sauce over the rolls, ensuring they are well covered.

Bake in the preheated oven for 25-30 minutes or until the rolls are golden brown.

Allow the Chocolate Pecan Caramel Rolls to cool slightly before serving.

Serve and enjoy these decadent and gooey rolls with a cup of coffee or tea!

Feel free to customize the recipe by adding extra chocolate chips or drizzling melted chocolate on top. Include any tips for achieving a soft and gooey texture in your cookbook. These Chocolate Pecan Caramel Rolls are a delightful treat for breakfast or dessert!

**Chocolate Hazelnut Muffins**

*Ingredients:*

- 2 cups all-purpose flour
- 1/2 cup unsweetened cocoa powder
- 1 tablespoon baking powder
- 1/2 teaspoon baking soda
- 1/2 teaspoon salt
- 1/2 cup unsalted butter, melted
- 1 cup granulated sugar
- 2 large eggs
- 1 teaspoon vanilla extract
- 1 cup buttermilk
- 1/2 cup chocolate hazelnut spread (such as Nutella)
- 1/2 cup chopped hazelnuts

*Instructions:*

Preheat your oven to 375°F (190°C). Line a muffin tin with paper liners.

In a bowl, whisk together the flour, cocoa powder, baking powder, baking soda, and salt.

In another bowl, cream together the melted butter and granulated sugar until well combined.

Add the eggs one at a time, beating well after each addition.

Stir in the vanilla extract.

Gradually add the dry ingredients to the wet ingredients, alternating with buttermilk. Begin and end with the dry ingredients, mixing until just combined.

Gently fold in the chocolate hazelnut spread and chopped hazelnuts until evenly distributed throughout the batter.

Spoon the batter into the prepared muffin tin, filling each cup about 2/3 full.

Bake in the preheated oven for 18-20 minutes or until a toothpick inserted into the center of a muffin comes out clean.

Allow the muffins to cool in the tin for a few minutes, then transfer them to a wire rack to cool completely.

Serve and enjoy these Chocolate Hazelnut Muffins as a delightful breakfast or snack!

Feel free to add a drizzle of melted chocolate or a sprinkle of chopped hazelnuts on top for extra indulgence. Include any tips for achieving a moist and flavorful texture in your cookbook. These Chocolate Hazelnut Muffins are a perfect combination of rich chocolate and nutty hazelnut flavors!

**Chocolate Raspberry Almond Cake**

*Ingredients:*

For the Cake:

- 1 cup unsalted butter, softened
- 1 cup granulated sugar
- 4 large eggs
- 1 teaspoon almond extract
- 1 cup all-purpose flour
- 1/2 cup almond flour
- 1/2 cup unsweetened cocoa powder
- 1 1/2 teaspoons baking powder
- 1/2 teaspoon baking soda
- 1/2 teaspoon salt
- 1 cup buttermilk

For the Raspberry Filling:

- 1 1/2 cups fresh raspberries
- 2 tablespoons granulated sugar
- 1 tablespoon lemon juice

For the Chocolate Ganache:

- 1/2 cup dark chocolate chips
- 1/4 cup heavy cream

For Garnish:

- Sliced almonds
- Fresh raspberries

*Instructions:*

For the Cake:

> Preheat your oven to 350°F (175°C). Grease and flour two 9-inch round cake pans.
> 
> In a large bowl, cream together the softened butter and granulated sugar until light and fluffy.
> 
> Add the eggs one at a time, beating well after each addition. Stir in the almond extract.
> 
> In a separate bowl, whisk together the all-purpose flour, almond flour, cocoa powder, baking powder, baking soda, and salt.
> 
> Gradually add the dry ingredients to the wet ingredients, alternating with buttermilk. Begin and end with the dry ingredients, mixing until just combined.
> 
> Divide the batter evenly between the prepared cake pans.
> 
> Bake in the preheated oven for 25-30 minutes or until a toothpick inserted into the center of the cakes comes out clean.
> 
> Allow the cakes to cool in the pans for 10 minutes, then transfer them to a wire rack to cool completely.

For the Raspberry Filling:

> In a saucepan, combine the fresh raspberries, granulated sugar, and lemon juice.

Cook over medium heat, stirring occasionally, until the raspberries break down and the mixture thickens.

Remove from heat and let it cool.

For the Chocolate Ganache:

In a heatproof bowl, combine the dark chocolate chips and heavy cream.

Heat the mixture in the microwave or on the stovetop until the chocolate is melted. Stir until smooth.

Assembly:

Place one cake layer on a serving plate.

Spread the raspberry filling over the top of the first cake layer.

Place the second cake layer on top.

Pour the chocolate ganache over the top of the cake, allowing it to drip down the sides.

Garnish with sliced almonds and fresh raspberries.

Chill the cake in the refrigerator for about 30 minutes to set the ganache.

Slice and serve this delectable Chocolate Raspberry Almond Cake!

Include any tips for achieving a moist and flavorful cake in your cookbook. This Chocolate Raspberry Almond Cake is a delightful combination of rich chocolate, nutty almond, and fruity raspberry flavors!

## Chocolate Coconut Ice Cream

*Ingredients:*

- 1 can (14 ounces) coconut milk (full-fat)
- 1 can (14 ounces) coconut cream
- 1/2 cup unsweetened cocoa powder
- 1/2 cup granulated sugar
- 1/4 cup maple syrup or agave nectar
- 1 teaspoon vanilla extract
- 1/2 cup shredded coconut (optional)
- 1/2 cup chocolate chunks or chips (optional)

*Instructions:*

In a blender, combine the coconut milk, coconut cream, cocoa powder, granulated sugar, maple syrup (or agave nectar), and vanilla extract.

Blend the ingredients until smooth and well combined.

If you have an ice cream maker, transfer the mixture to the machine and churn according to the manufacturer's instructions.

If you don't have an ice cream maker, pour the mixture into a freezer-safe container.

If using, stir in the shredded coconut and chocolate chunks.

Cover the container and place it in the freezer.

Every 30 minutes for the first few hours, stir the ice cream with a fork to break up ice crystals.

Continue freezing until the ice cream reaches your desired consistency, usually 4-6 hours.

Once fully frozen, scoop the Chocolate Coconut Ice Cream into bowls or cones. Serve and enjoy this creamy and dairy-free treat!

Feel free to customize the recipe by adding your favorite mix-ins, such as chopped nuts or swirls of chocolate sauce. Include any tips for achieving a creamy texture and preventing ice crystals in your cookbook. This Chocolate Coconut Ice Cream is a delightful and refreshing dessert for chocolate and coconut lovers!

## Chocolate Covered Macadamia Nuts

*Ingredients:*

- 1 cup macadamia nuts
- 1 cup semisweet or dark chocolate chips
- 1 tablespoon coconut oil (optional)
- Sea salt for sprinkling (optional)

*Instructions:*

Line a baking sheet with parchment paper.

In a heatproof bowl, melt the chocolate chips in the microwave or using a double boiler. If desired, add coconut oil to achieve a smoother consistency.

Stir the melted chocolate until smooth.

Using a fork or chocolate dipping tool, dip each macadamia nut into the melted chocolate, coating it evenly.

Lift the chocolate-covered nut, allowing any excess chocolate to drip off.

Place the chocolate-covered macadamia nut on the prepared baking sheet.

Repeat the process for the remaining macadamia nuts.

If desired, sprinkle a pinch of sea salt over the chocolate-covered nuts while the chocolate is still wet.

Allow the chocolate to set. You can place the baking sheet in the refrigerator for quicker setting.

Once set, transfer the Chocolate Covered Macadamia Nuts to a serving plate or store in an airtight container.

Serve and enjoy these delightful and indulgent treats!

Feel free to experiment with different types of chocolate or add a drizzle of white chocolate for extra flair. Include any tips for achieving a smooth chocolate coating and preventing the nuts from clumping in your cookbook. These Chocolate Covered Macadamia Nuts make for a luxurious and satisfying snack!

**Chocolate Banana Pancakes**

*Ingredients:*

- 1 cup all-purpose flour
- 2 tablespoons cocoa powder
- 2 tablespoons granulated sugar
- 1 teaspoon baking powder
- 1/2 teaspoon baking soda
- 1/4 teaspoon salt
- 1 cup buttermilk
- 1 large ripe banana, mashed
- 1 large egg
- 2 tablespoons unsalted butter, melted
- 1/2 cup chocolate chips
- Cooking spray or additional butter for greasing the griddle

*Instructions:*

In a large bowl, whisk together the flour, cocoa powder, sugar, baking powder, baking soda, and salt.

In a separate bowl, whisk together the buttermilk, mashed banana, egg, and melted butter.

Pour the wet ingredients into the dry ingredients and stir until just combined. Do not overmix; a few lumps are okay.

Gently fold in the chocolate chips.

Preheat a griddle or non-stick skillet over medium heat. Lightly grease with cooking spray or butter.

Pour 1/4 cup portions of batter onto the griddle for each pancake.

Cook until bubbles form on the surface of the pancake, then flip and cook the other side until golden brown.

Repeat with the remaining batter.

Serve the Chocolate Banana Pancakes warm, topped with additional sliced bananas, chocolate chips, or a drizzle of maple syrup.

Enjoy this delightful and decadent breakfast treat!

Include any tips for achieving fluffy and flavorful pancakes in your cookbook. These Chocolate Banana Pancakes are a perfect combination of rich chocolate and sweet banana flavors!

**Chocolate Mint Oreo Truffles**

*Ingredients:*

- 1 package (about 36) Mint Oreo cookies
- 8 ounces cream cheese, softened
- 1 teaspoon peppermint extract
- 12 ounces green candy melts or chocolate chips
- Crushed candy canes or sprinkles for decoration (optional)

*Instructions:*

Place the Mint Oreo cookies in a food processor and pulse until you have fine crumbs.

In a large mixing bowl, combine the Oreo crumbs with softened cream cheese and peppermint extract. Mix until well combined and smooth.

Line a baking sheet with parchment paper.

Scoop out small portions of the Oreo mixture and roll them into bite-sized truffle balls. Place them on the prepared baking sheet.

Chill the truffle balls in the refrigerator for at least 30 minutes to firm up.

In a heatproof bowl, melt the green candy melts or chocolate chips according to the package instructions.

Using a fork or toothpick, dip each chilled truffle ball into the melted chocolate, coating it evenly. Allow any excess chocolate to drip off.

Place the coated truffle back on the parchment-lined baking sheet.

If desired, sprinkle crushed candy canes or festive sprinkles on top of the truffles while the chocolate is still wet.

Repeat the dipping process for the remaining truffle balls.

Allow the chocolate coating to set. You can place the baking sheet in the refrigerator for quicker setting.

Once set, transfer the Chocolate Mint Oreo Truffles to a serving plate or store in an airtight container.

Serve and enjoy these delightful and minty truffles!

Feel free to customize the recipe by using different types of Oreo cookies or decorations. Include any tips for achieving a smooth chocolate coating and creating festive presentations in your cookbook. These Chocolate Mint Oreo Truffles make for a delicious and festive treat!

**Chocolate Hazelnut Pancakes**

*Ingredients:*

- 1 cup all-purpose flour
- 2 tablespoons unsweetened cocoa powder
- 2 tablespoons granulated sugar
- 1 teaspoon baking powder
- 1/2 teaspoon baking soda
- 1/4 teaspoon salt
- 1 cup buttermilk
- 1 large egg
- 2 tablespoons unsalted butter, melted
- 1/4 cup chocolate hazelnut spread (such as Nutella)
- Hazelnuts, chopped, for garnish (optional)
- Maple syrup for serving

*Instructions:*

In a large bowl, whisk together the flour, cocoa powder, sugar, baking powder, baking soda, and salt.

In a separate bowl, whisk together the buttermilk, egg, and melted butter.

Pour the wet ingredients into the dry ingredients and stir until just combined. Do not overmix; a few lumps are okay.

Gently fold in the chocolate hazelnut spread until swirls appear in the batter.

Preheat a griddle or non-stick skillet over medium heat. Lightly grease with cooking spray or butter.

Pour 1/4 cup portions of batter onto the griddle for each pancake.

Cook until bubbles form on the surface of the pancake, then flip and cook the other side until golden brown.

Repeat with the remaining batter.

Garnish the Chocolate Hazelnut Pancakes with chopped hazelnuts if desired.

Serve the pancakes warm, drizzled with maple syrup.

Enjoy this delightful and indulgent breakfast treat!

Include any tips for achieving fluffy and flavorful pancakes in your cookbook. These Chocolate Hazelnut Pancakes are a perfect blend of rich chocolate and nutty hazelnut flavors!

**Chocolate Raspberry Ice Cream**

*Ingredients:*

- 2 cups fresh or frozen raspberries
- 1/2 cup granulated sugar
- 2 tablespoons lemon juice
- 2 cups heavy cream
- 1 cup whole milk
- 1 cup semisweet chocolate chips or chopped chocolate
- 1 teaspoon vanilla extract

*Instructions:*

In a blender or food processor, puree the raspberries until smooth.

Strain the raspberry puree through a fine-mesh sieve to remove the seeds, collecting the smooth raspberry juice in a bowl.

In a saucepan over medium heat, combine the raspberry juice, granulated sugar, and lemon juice. Cook, stirring occasionally, until the sugar dissolves and the mixture is well combined. Remove from heat and let it cool.

In a separate bowl, whisk together the heavy cream, whole milk, and vanilla extract.

Add the cooled raspberry mixture to the cream mixture and whisk until well combined.

Refrigerate the mixture for at least 2 hours or until thoroughly chilled.

Once chilled, pour the mixture into an ice cream maker and churn according to the manufacturer's instructions.

In the last few minutes of churning, add the chocolate chips or chopped chocolate to evenly distribute throughout the ice cream.

Transfer the churned ice cream to a lidded container and freeze for an additional 4-6 hours or until firm.

Scoop and serve this delightful Chocolate Raspberry Ice Cream!

Feel free to garnish with additional raspberries or a drizzle of chocolate sauce when serving. Include any tips for achieving a creamy texture and maximizing raspberry flavor in your cookbook. This Chocolate Raspberry Ice Cream is a refreshing and decadent treat!

**Chocolate Almond Joy Smoothie**

*Ingredients:*

- 1 cup almond milk
- 1 ripe banana, peeled and frozen
- 2 tablespoons unsweetened cocoa powder
- 2 tablespoons shredded coconut
- 2 tablespoons almond butter
- 1 tablespoon chocolate chips or chopped chocolate
- 1/2 teaspoon almond extract
- Ice cubes (optional)
- Sweetener to taste (such as honey or maple syrup, optional)

*Instructions:*

In a blender, combine the almond milk, frozen banana, cocoa powder, shredded coconut, almond butter, chocolate chips, and almond extract.

If desired, add ice cubes for a colder and thicker smoothie.

Blend the ingredients until smooth and creamy.

Taste the smoothie and add sweetener if needed, depending on your preference.

Pour the Chocolate Almond Joy Smoothie into a glass.

Garnish with additional shredded coconut or chocolate chips if desired.

Serve and enjoy this delightful and indulgent smoothie!

Feel free to customize the recipe by adding a scoop of protein powder or adjusting the ingredients to suit your taste. Include any tips for achieving a well-balanced and satisfying smoothie in your cookbook. This Chocolate Almond Joy Smoothie is a delicious and healthier way to enjoy the flavors of the classic candy bar!

**Chocolate Tiramisu Cupcakes**

*Ingredients:*

For the Cupcakes:

- 1 cup all-purpose flour
- 1/2 cup cocoa powder
- 1 teaspoon baking powder
- 1/2 teaspoon baking soda
- 1/4 teaspoon salt
- 1/2 cup unsalted butter, softened
- 1 cup granulated sugar
- 2 large eggs
- 1 teaspoon vanilla extract
- 1 cup buttermilk

For the Coffee Soaking Syrup:

- 1/2 cup brewed strong coffee, cooled
- 2 tablespoons coffee liqueur (e.g., Kahlúa)
- 2 tablespoons granulated sugar

For the Tiramisu Filling:

- 8 ounces mascarpone cheese, softened
- 1/2 cup powdered sugar
- 1 teaspoon vanilla extract

- 1 cup heavy cream, whipped to stiff peaks

For the Chocolate Ganache:

- 1/2 cup semisweet chocolate chips
- 1/4 cup heavy cream

*Instructions:*

For the Cupcakes:

Preheat your oven to 350°F (175°C). Line a muffin tin with cupcake liners.

In a bowl, whisk together the flour, cocoa powder, baking powder, baking soda, and salt.

In a separate large bowl, cream together the softened butter and granulated sugar until light and fluffy.

Add the eggs one at a time, beating well after each addition. Stir in the vanilla extract.

Gradually add the dry ingredients to the wet ingredients, alternating with buttermilk. Begin and end with the dry ingredients, mixing until just combined.

Divide the batter evenly among the cupcake liners.

Bake in the preheated oven for 18-20 minutes or until a toothpick inserted into the center of a cupcake comes out clean.

Allow the cupcakes to cool in the tin for 10 minutes, then transfer them to a wire rack to cool completely.

For the Coffee Soaking Syrup:

In a bowl, combine the brewed coffee, coffee liqueur, and granulated sugar. Stir until the sugar dissolves.

For the Tiramisu Filling:

In a mixing bowl, beat together the mascarpone cheese, powdered sugar, and vanilla extract until smooth.

Gently fold in the whipped cream until well combined.

Assembly:

Using a sharp knife, cut a small cone-shaped piece out of the center of each cupcake.

Dip the top of each cupcake into the coffee soaking syrup.

Fill the holes with the tiramisu filling.

For the Chocolate Ganache:

In a heatproof bowl, combine the chocolate chips and heavy cream.

Heat the mixture in the microwave or on the stovetop until the chocolate is melted. Stir until smooth.

Allow the ganache to cool slightly.

Drizzle the chocolate ganache over the filled cupcakes.

Refrigerate the cupcakes for at least 1-2 hours before serving.

Serve and enjoy these decadent Chocolate Tiramisu Cupcakes!

Feel free to garnish with a dusting of cocoa powder or chocolate shavings. Include any tips for assembling and storing these delightful cupcakes in your cookbook. These Chocolate Tiramisu Cupcakes are a delightful twist on the classic Italian dessert!

**Chocolate Coconut Cream Pie**

*Ingredients:*

For the Pie Crust:

- 1 1/2 cups chocolate cookie crumbs
- 1/4 cup unsalted butter, melted

For the Chocolate Ganache Layer:

- 1 cup semisweet chocolate chips
- 1/2 cup heavy cream

For the Coconut Cream Filling:

- 1 cup sweetened shredded coconut
- 2 cups whole milk
- 1 cup canned coconut milk
- 3/4 cup granulated sugar
- 1/4 cup cornstarch
- 1/4 teaspoon salt
- 4 large egg yolks, beaten
- 2 tablespoons unsalted butter
- 1 teaspoon vanilla extract

For the Whipped Cream Topping:

- 1 cup heavy cream

- 2 tablespoons powdered sugar
- 1/2 teaspoon vanilla extract
- Additional shredded coconut for garnish (optional)

*Instructions:*

For the Pie Crust:

Preheat your oven to 350°F (175°C).

In a bowl, combine the chocolate cookie crumbs and melted butter. Press the mixture into the bottom and up the sides of a 9-inch pie dish to form the crust.

Bake the crust in the preheated oven for 8-10 minutes. Allow it to cool completely.

For the Chocolate Ganache Layer:

In a heatproof bowl, combine the chocolate chips and heavy cream.

Heat the mixture in the microwave or on the stovetop until the chocolate is melted. Stir until smooth.

Pour the chocolate ganache into the cooled pie crust, spreading it evenly. Allow it to set.

For the Coconut Cream Filling:

In a skillet over medium heat, toast the shredded coconut until golden brown. Set aside.

In a saucepan, combine the whole milk, canned coconut milk, granulated sugar, cornstarch, and salt. Whisk until well combined.

Cook the mixture over medium heat, stirring constantly, until it thickens.

In a separate bowl, beat the egg yolks. Gradually whisk in about 1 cup of the hot milk mixture to temper the eggs.

Pour the egg mixture back into the saucepan, whisking continuously.

Continue cooking until the filling reaches a pudding-like consistency.

Remove from heat and stir in the toasted shredded coconut, butter, and vanilla extract.

Pour the coconut cream filling over the chocolate ganache layer in the pie crust.

Refrigerate the pie for at least 4 hours or until set.

For the Whipped Cream Topping:

In a chilled bowl, whip the heavy cream, powdered sugar, and vanilla extract until stiff peaks form.

Spread the whipped cream over the chilled coconut cream filling.

Garnish with additional shredded coconut if desired.

Refrigerate for an additional 1-2 hours before serving.

Slice and enjoy this decadent Chocolate Coconut Cream Pie!

Include any tips for achieving a smooth and luscious coconut cream filling in your cookbook. This Chocolate Coconut Cream Pie is a delightful combination of rich chocolate and tropical coconut flavors!

**Chocolate Raspberry Danish**

*Ingredients:*

For the Dough:

- 2 1/4 teaspoons (1 packet) active dry yeast
- 1/4 cup warm water (about 110°F or 43°C)
- 1/2 cup milk, warmed
- 1/4 cup granulated sugar
- 1/2 cup unsalted butter, softened
- 1/2 teaspoon salt
- 2 large eggs
- 3 cups all-purpose flour

For the Filling:

- 1/2 cup raspberry jam or preserves
- 1/2 cup chocolate chips or chopped chocolate
- 1/4 cup slivered almonds (optional)

For the Glaze:

- 1 cup powdered sugar
- 2 tablespoons milk
- 1/2 teaspoon vanilla extract

*Instructions:*

For the Dough:

In a small bowl, combine the warm water and yeast. Let it sit for about 5 minutes until foamy.

In a large mixing bowl, combine the warmed milk, granulated sugar, softened butter, salt, and eggs. Mix well.

Add the activated yeast mixture to the bowl and mix again.

Gradually add the flour, one cup at a time, mixing well after each addition.

Continue adding flour until the dough comes together.

Turn the dough onto a floured surface and knead for about 5-7 minutes or until it becomes smooth and elastic.

Place the dough in a greased bowl, cover with a kitchen towel, and let it rise in a warm place for 1-1.5 hours or until it doubles in size.

Assembly:

Preheat your oven to 375°F (190°C) and line a baking sheet with parchment paper.

Punch down the risen dough and roll it out into a rectangle on a floured surface.

Spread raspberry jam evenly over the dough, leaving a border around the edges.

Sprinkle chocolate chips or chopped chocolate over the raspberry jam.

Roll the dough tightly from one long side to the other, forming a log.

Slice the log into 12 equal pieces.

Place the slices on the prepared baking sheet, leaving space between each.

Optionally, sprinkle slivered almonds on top.

Bake in the preheated oven for 18-20 minutes or until the danishes are golden brown.

For the Glaze:

In a bowl, whisk together powdered sugar, milk, and vanilla extract until smooth.

Drizzle the glaze over the warm danishes.

Allow the glaze to set before serving.

Serve and enjoy these delightful Chocolate Raspberry Danishes!

Include any tips for achieving a soft and flaky dough in your cookbook. These Chocolate Raspberry Danishes are a perfect combination of sweet raspberry, rich chocolate, and buttery pastry!

**Chocolate Mint Thumbprint Cookies**

*Ingredients:*

For the Cookies:

- 1 cup unsalted butter, softened
- 1 cup granulated sugar
- 1 large egg
- 1 teaspoon vanilla extract
- 2 cups all-purpose flour
- 1/2 cup unsweetened cocoa powder
- 1/4 teaspoon salt

For the Mint Filling:

- 1 cup powdered sugar
- 2 tablespoons unsalted butter, softened
- 1 tablespoon milk
- 1/2 teaspoon peppermint extract
- Green food coloring (optional)
- Chocolate ganache (store-bought or homemade) for filling

*Instructions:*

For the Cookies:

> Preheat your oven to 350°F (175°C). Line a baking sheet with parchment paper.

In a large bowl, cream together the softened butter and granulated sugar until light and fluffy.

Add the egg and vanilla extract, and beat until well combined.

In a separate bowl, whisk together the flour, cocoa powder, and salt.

Gradually add the dry ingredients to the wet ingredients, mixing until the dough comes together.

Shape the dough into 1-inch balls and place them on the prepared baking sheet.

Use your thumb or the back of a small spoon to make an indentation in the center of each cookie.

Bake in the preheated oven for 10-12 minutes or until the cookies are set.

Remove from the oven and gently press down the center of each cookie again if needed.

Allow the cookies to cool on the baking sheet for a few minutes before transferring them to a wire rack to cool completely.

For the Mint Filling:

In a bowl, beat together the powdered sugar, softened butter, milk, peppermint extract, and green food coloring (if using) until smooth.

Once the cookies are completely cooled, fill each indentation with a small amount of mint filling.

Optionally, melt chocolate ganache and drizzle over the mint filling.

Allow the mint filling and chocolate to set before serving.

Serve and enjoy these delightful Chocolate Mint Thumbprint Cookies!

Include any tips for achieving a perfect thumbprint and creating a smooth mint filling in your cookbook. These Chocolate Mint Thumbprint Cookies are a festive and minty treat for any occasion!

**Chocolate Pecan Pie Milkshake**

*Ingredients:*

- 2 cups vanilla ice cream
- 1/2 cup chopped pecan pie (homemade or store-bought)
- 1/4 cup pecans, chopped and toasted
- 1/2 cup whole milk
- 2 tablespoons chocolate syrup
- Whipped cream for topping
- Additional chopped pecans for garnish (optional)

*Instructions:*

In a blender, combine the vanilla ice cream, chopped pecan pie, toasted pecans, whole milk, and chocolate syrup.

Blend the ingredients until smooth and creamy.

Pour the milkshake into glasses.

Top each milkshake with a generous dollop of whipped cream.

If desired, garnish with additional chopped pecans.

Serve immediately and enjoy this indulgent Chocolate Pecan Pie Milkshake!

Feel free to customize the recipe by adding a drizzle of caramel sauce or a sprinkle of cinnamon. Include any tips for achieving a rich and flavorful milkshake in your cookbook. This Chocolate Pecan Pie Milkshake is a delightful way to enjoy the flavors of pecan pie in a cool and refreshing drink!

**Chocolate Hazelnut Cheesecake**

*Ingredients:*

For the Crust:

- 1 1/2 cups chocolate cookie crumbs
- 1/4 cup unsalted butter, melted

For the Filling:

- 24 ounces cream cheese, softened
- 1 cup granulated sugar
- 3 large eggs
- 1 cup hazelnut chocolate spread (such as Nutella)
- 1 teaspoon vanilla extract
- 1/2 cup all-purpose flour

For the Topping:

- 1/2 cup hazelnuts, chopped and toasted
- 1/4 cup chocolate hazelnut spread, melted

*Instructions:*

For the Crust:

>Preheat your oven to 325°F (163°C). Grease a 9-inch springform pan.
>
>In a bowl, combine the chocolate cookie crumbs and melted butter. Press the mixture into the bottom of the prepared pan to form the crust.

Bake the crust in the preheated oven for 10 minutes. Allow it to cool while preparing the filling.

## For the Filling:

In a large bowl, beat the softened cream cheese and granulated sugar until smooth.

Add the eggs one at a time, beating well after each addition.

Mix in the hazelnut chocolate spread and vanilla extract until well combined.

Gradually add the flour, mixing until just combined.

Pour the filling over the cooled crust in the springform pan.

## Baking the Cheesecake:

Bake in the preheated oven for 55-65 minutes or until the center is set and the top is lightly browned.

Allow the cheesecake to cool completely in the pan on a wire rack.

Refrigerate the cheesecake for at least 4 hours or overnight.

## For the Topping:

Toast the chopped hazelnuts in a dry skillet over medium heat until lightly browned. Allow them to cool.

Drizzle the melted chocolate hazelnut spread over the chilled cheesecake.

Sprinkle the toasted hazelnuts on top.

Return the cheesecake to the refrigerator to allow the topping to set.

Once set, release the sides of the springform pan and transfer the cheesecake to a serving plate.

Slice and enjoy this decadent Chocolate Hazelnut Cheesecake!

Include any tips for achieving a creamy and luscious cheesecake texture in your cookbook. This Chocolate Hazelnut Cheesecake is a delightful combination of rich chocolate and nutty hazelnut flavors!

**Chocolate Cherry Almond Granola**

*Ingredients:*

- 3 cups old-fashioned rolled oats
- 1 cup almonds, chopped
- 1/2 cup unsweetened shredded coconut
- 1/4 cup cocoa powder
- 1/2 teaspoon ground cinnamon
- 1/4 teaspoon salt
- 1/2 cup coconut oil, melted
- 1/3 cup honey or maple syrup
- 1 teaspoon vanilla extract
- 1 cup dried cherries, chopped
- 1/2 cup dark chocolate chips or chunks

*Instructions:*

Preheat your oven to 325°F (163°C). Line a baking sheet with parchment paper.

In a large bowl, combine the rolled oats, chopped almonds, shredded coconut, cocoa powder, ground cinnamon, and salt.

In a separate bowl, whisk together the melted coconut oil, honey or maple syrup, and vanilla extract.

Pour the wet ingredients over the dry ingredients and stir until the mixture is well coated.

Spread the granola mixture evenly onto the prepared baking sheet.

Bake in the preheated oven for 20-25 minutes, stirring once halfway through, or until the granola is golden brown and fragrant.

Remove the granola from the oven and let it cool completely on the baking sheet.

Once cooled, stir in the chopped dried cherries and dark chocolate chips or chunks.

Transfer the Chocolate Cherry Almond Granola to an airtight container for storage.

Serve with yogurt, milk, or enjoy it as a snack on its own.

Include any tips for achieving a crunchy and flavorful granola in your cookbook. This Chocolate Cherry Almond Granola is a delightful combination of rich chocolate, sweet cherries, and nutty almonds!

**Chocolate Orange Ricotta Pancakes**

*Ingredients:*

- 1 cup all-purpose flour
- 2 tablespoons cocoa powder
- 2 tablespoons granulated sugar
- 1 teaspoon baking powder
- 1/2 teaspoon baking soda
- 1/4 teaspoon salt
- 1 cup ricotta cheese
- 2/3 cup milk
- 2 large eggs
- Zest of 1 orange
- 2 tablespoons fresh orange juice
- 1/2 cup chocolate chips
- Butter or oil for cooking
- Maple syrup and additional chocolate chips for serving

*Instructions:*

In a large bowl, whisk together the flour, cocoa powder, sugar, baking powder, baking soda, and salt.

In another bowl, combine the ricotta cheese, milk, eggs, orange zest, and orange juice. Mix until well combined.

Pour the wet ingredients into the dry ingredients and stir until just combined. Be careful not to overmix; a few lumps are okay.

Gently fold in the chocolate chips.

Heat a griddle or non-stick skillet over medium heat. Add a small amount of butter or oil to coat the surface.

Pour 1/4 cup portions of batter onto the griddle for each pancake.

Cook until bubbles form on the surface of the pancake, then flip and cook the other side until golden brown.

Repeat with the remaining batter.

Serve the Chocolate Orange Ricotta Pancakes warm, topped with maple syrup and additional chocolate chips.

Enjoy these delightful and flavorful pancakes!

Include any tips for achieving fluffy and chocolatey pancakes in your cookbook. These Chocolate Orange Ricotta Pancakes are a perfect blend of rich chocolate, citrusy orange, and creamy ricotta flavors!

**Chocolate Raspberry Popsicles**

*Ingredients:*

- 1 cup fresh raspberries
- 1/4 cup granulated sugar
- 1 tablespoon lemon juice
- 1 cup chocolate milk (store-bought or homemade)
- 1/2 cup plain Greek yogurt
- 1/4 cup chocolate chips or chopped chocolate

*Instructions:*

In a blender, combine the fresh raspberries, granulated sugar, and lemon juice. Blend until smooth.

Strain the raspberry mixture through a fine-mesh sieve to remove the seeds, collecting the raspberry puree in a bowl.

In a separate bowl, whisk together the chocolate milk and plain Greek yogurt until well combined.

Fill each popsicle mold by alternating layers of the raspberry puree and chocolate yogurt mixture.

After each layer, sprinkle a few chocolate chips or chopped chocolate.

Insert popsicle sticks into the molds.

Freeze the popsicles for at least 4-6 hours or until completely frozen.

Once frozen, remove the popsicles from the molds by running them under warm water for a few seconds.

Serve and enjoy these refreshing Chocolate Raspberry Popsicles!

Feel free to customize the recipe by adjusting the sweetness to your liking or adding more chocolate chips for extra indulgence. Include any tips for creating layers and achieving a perfect texture in your cookbook. These Chocolate Raspberry Popsicles are a delightful treat for hot days!

**Chocolate Banana Split**

*Ingredients:*

- 3 ripe bananas, split lengthwise
- 3 scoops vanilla ice cream
- 3 scoops chocolate ice cream
- 3 scoops strawberry ice cream
- Chocolate sauce
- Strawberry sauce
- Pineapple chunks
- Chopped nuts (such as walnuts or almonds)
- Whipped cream
- Maraschino cherries
- Sprinkles

*Instructions:*

Place the split bananas in a long dish or on a banana split boat.

Scoop vanilla, chocolate, and strawberry ice cream between the banana halves.

Drizzle chocolate sauce, strawberry sauce, and pineapple chunks over the ice cream.

Sprinkle chopped nuts over the top.

Add dollops of whipped cream on each scoop of ice cream.

Garnish with maraschino cherries on top.

Finish by sprinkling colorful sprinkles over the entire banana split.

Serve immediately and enjoy this indulgent Chocolate Banana Split!

Feel free to customize the toppings based on personal preferences. Include any tips for creating a visually appealing and delicious banana split in your cookbook. This Chocolate Banana Split is a classic dessert that's sure to delight!

**Chocolate Mint Panna Cotta**

*Ingredients:*

- 2 cups heavy cream
- 1/2 cup granulated sugar
- 4 ounces dark chocolate, finely chopped
- 1 teaspoon peppermint extract
- 1 teaspoon vanilla extract
- 1 packet (2 1/4 teaspoons) unflavored gelatin
- 3 tablespoons cold water
- Fresh mint leaves for garnish (optional)

*Instructions:*

In a saucepan, heat the heavy cream and sugar over medium heat until it just begins to simmer. Do not boil.

Remove the saucepan from heat and add the finely chopped dark chocolate. Stir until the chocolate is completely melted and the mixture is smooth.

Stir in the peppermint extract and vanilla extract until well combined.

In a small bowl, sprinkle the unflavored gelatin over the cold water. Let it sit for a few minutes to bloom.

After blooming, gently heat the gelatin mixture in the microwave or on the stovetop until it becomes liquid. Make sure it is well dissolved.

Pour the gelatin mixture into the chocolate and cream mixture, stirring continuously.

Strain the mixture through a fine-mesh sieve to ensure a smooth texture.

Divide the chocolate mint mixture among serving glasses or molds.

Refrigerate for at least 4 hours or until the panna cotta is set.

Once set, garnish with fresh mint leaves if desired.

Serve and enjoy this elegant Chocolate Mint Panna Cotta!

Include any tips for achieving a silky-smooth texture and perfect set in your cookbook.

This Chocolate Mint Panna Cotta is a delightful and refreshing dessert for any occasion!

**Chocolate Pecan Pralines**

*Ingredients:*

- 1 cup pecan halves
- 1 cup granulated sugar
- 1/2 cup packed light brown sugar
- 1/2 cup heavy cream
- 1/4 cup unsalted butter
- 1/4 cup cocoa powder
- 1/4 teaspoon salt
- 1 teaspoon vanilla extract

*Instructions:*

Line a baking sheet with parchment paper or a silicone baking mat. Set aside.

In a dry skillet over medium heat, toast the pecan halves until fragrant and slightly browned. Be careful not to burn them. Remove from heat and set aside.

In a heavy-bottomed saucepan, combine granulated sugar, brown sugar, heavy cream, unsalted butter, cocoa powder, and salt.

Cook over medium heat, stirring constantly until the sugar dissolves and the mixture comes to a boil.

Once boiling, clip a candy thermometer to the side of the saucepan. Continue cooking without stirring until the temperature reaches 235°F (113°C) - soft ball stage.

Remove the saucepan from heat and let it sit undisturbed for a couple of minutes to cool slightly.

Stir in the vanilla extract and toasted pecan halves.

Quickly drop spoonfuls of the mixture onto the prepared baking sheet.

Allow the pralines to cool and harden at room temperature.

Once fully set, store the Chocolate Pecan Pralines in an airtight container.

Enjoy these sweet and nutty treats!

Include any tips for achieving the right consistency and flavor in your cookbook. These Chocolate Pecan Pralines are a delightful combination of rich chocolate, caramel, and toasted pecans!

**Chocolate Hazelnut Granola Bars**

*Ingredients:*

- 2 cups old-fashioned rolled oats
- 1 cup chopped hazelnuts
- 1/2 cup honey
- 1/4 cup unsalted butter
- 1/4 cup brown sugar, packed
- 1/3 cup chocolate hazelnut spread (such as Nutella)
- 1 teaspoon vanilla extract
- 1/4 teaspoon salt
- 1/2 cup mini chocolate chips

*Instructions:*

Preheat your oven to 350°F (175°C). Line a square baking pan with parchment paper, leaving an overhang on two opposite sides.

In a large mixing bowl, combine the rolled oats and chopped hazelnuts.

In a saucepan over medium heat, combine honey, butter, and brown sugar. Stir until the butter and sugar are melted.

Remove the saucepan from heat and stir in the chocolate hazelnut spread, vanilla extract, and salt until well combined.

Pour the wet mixture over the oats and hazelnuts. Stir until the dry ingredients are well coated.

Fold in the mini chocolate chips.

Transfer the mixture to the prepared baking pan and press it down evenly.

Bake in the preheated oven for 15-18 minutes or until the edges are golden brown.

Allow the granola bars to cool completely in the pan.

Once cooled, use the parchment paper overhang to lift the granola slab out of the pan.

Cut into bars or squares.

Store the Chocolate Hazelnut Granola Bars in an airtight container.

Enjoy these delicious and nutty granola bars as a snack or breakfast treat!

Include any tips for achieving the right balance of sweetness and crunch in your cookbook. These Chocolate Hazelnut Granola Bars are a perfect combination of wholesome oats, crunchy hazelnuts, and sweet chocolate hazelnut goodness!

www.ingramcontent.com/pod-product-compliance
Lightning Source LLC
LaVergne TN
LVHW061935070526
838199LV00060B/3834